Also by the author

*Speaking Volumes: Conversations with Remarkable Writers*

*Samovar*

*Jewish Cooking, Jewish Cooks*

*The Best Australian Essays 2011* (editor)

*The Best Australian Essays 2012* (editor)

Ramona Koval is a writer, journalist and broadcaster. She presented ABC Radio National's *The Book Show* and *Books and Writing*, which were broadcast across Australia and throughout the world between 1995 and 2011. She blogs at ramonakoval.com

# RAMONA KOVAL

## BY THE BOOK

### A READER'S GUIDE TO LIFE

TEXT PUBLISHING
MELBOURNE AUSTRALIA

*For my five little readers—Maya, Eden, Bella,*
*Amelia and Jesse—with love*

The paper used in this book is manufactured only from wood grown in
sustainable regrowth forests.

textpublishing.com.au

The Text Publishing Company
Swann House
22 William Street
Melbourne Victoria 3000
Australia

Published in 2012 by The Text Publishing Company
An earlier draft of sections of chapter 1 and chapter 4 was published in
*Overland*; chapter 11, in the *Age*: chapter 14, in *The Best Australian Essays
2004* and the Canadian literary journal *Brick*.

Cover design by WH Chong
Page design by Imogen Stubbs
Typeset by J&M Typesetting

Printed and bound in Australia by Griffin Press an Accredited ISO AS/
NZS 14001:2004 Environmental Management System printer

National Library of Australia Cataloguing-in-Publication entry:
Author: Koval, Ramona, 1954-
Title: By the book : a reader's guide to life / by Ramona Koval.
ISBN: 9781922079060 (hbk.)
ISBN: 9781921961311 (ebook.)
Subjects: Koval, Ramona, 1954—Books and reading.
Books and reading.
Authors.
Dewey Number: 028.9.

# CONTENTS

## CHAPTER I

# High above the city

Reading a book, my mother would stretch out in our lounge room on one of the deep purple divans that would be made up later into beds, her soft body covered in a blanket, her attention absorbed by the pages in her hands. She was lost to us.

I'm sure she must have read aloud to me, a soft Polish lilt to her voice, but I can't remember Mama doing this. Reading was her self-education program, and English was the latest in a line of language lessons that had started with Yiddish in the Polish shtetl where she had been born, then Polish when she was big enough to go to school at seven, then German when she was living under a false identity as a teenager in Warsaw during the war (carefully hiding the Yiddish construction and accent, which had their roots in

Middle German), then French when she lived in Paris for four years after the war. Now we were in Melbourne, and the pages she read on the couch with such concentration were usually in English.

Her name was Sara. Before I was born she worked as a 'finisher' in a garment factory in Flinders Lane, in the heart of the city's rag-trade, sewing on buttons by hand and embroidering collars. She had deep blue eyes and wavy brown hair, which she said had been blonde like mine but turned dark after having me. She was on the short side, with a full bosom, as they said then, and rounded hips. She wore a starched apron in our small one-bedroom, ground-floor flat, but would always take it off to go outside. She had little to spend on herself, but she favoured a particular brand of French perfume, Amour Amour by Jean Patou. I suspect she didn't buy it for herself. And that my father certainly wouldn't have thought of giving it to her.

I can't remember a proper bookshelf in our flat, so perhaps in those early years my mother borrowed her books from friends, although I don't think of any of them as readers. I don't remember going to a library till much later.

By the time I was three, in 1957, I owned some Little Golden Books. Now the only one I recognise is *The Little Red Hen*, the story of an industrious hen that tries to enlist the other farmyard animals to help with planting, harvesting, and otherwise preparing the grain for flour to be made into bread. They are too busy having fun, and when her hard work is rewarded she doesn't share her bounty with them.

I have always thought the little red hen was a twisted martyr who should have made the tasks fun so the other animals might have wanted to help her. The Little Golden Books were targeted at exactly the child I was. Published in war-time America, in 1942, they were twenty-five cents each and were designed to appeal to children from all socioeconomic levels. They were sold broadly, in department stores as well as bookshops and specialist children's outlets. In 1950s working-class Melbourne, we bought our books from the newsagent.

Enid Blyton's *Noddy Goes to Toyland* was another favourite. I remember the warm tangerine cover and the happily skewed multicoloured letters of the title. I couldn't read yet. I liked Noddy and Big Ears because they had a red open-topped car. They used it to breeze about the countryside and get away from evil golliwogs. That's what reading was for my mother, and became for me—a way to escape, a private time machine, a place that began with moral instruction but soon morphed into empathy and imagination.

When I went to kindergarten at four, I discovered that there was more than one Noddy book—the bookshelf there had lots of them: *Here Comes Noddy Again, Be*

*Brave Little Noddy!, Do Look Out Noddy!* and *Noddy Gets into Trouble*. I learned that books could be collected, that they were important enough to keep and that a story that seemed to be over could be part of a bigger one.

I tackled the *John and Betty* books. They were full of mysterious symbols to be mastered but, when you did, their messages were so much less interesting than Toytown and Mr Plod.

John can jump. Betty can jump too. Fluff the cat and Scottie the dog likewise.

I had chickenpox that year and was away from kindergarten for some weeks. When I came back it was my turn to read aloud. I loved my teacher, Miss Joseph, who was large and warm and towered over the little children. I wanted to make her happy. There was a new letter at the front of a group of sentences. It looked like the letter *l* for lamp and lady and lolly. So I spoke up loudly. L can see Scottie. L can see Fluff. There was a murmuring as I charged ahead. L can see John. L can see Betty.

Miss Joseph asked me to stop. That's not L, she said, it's capital I. It means *I* as in 'I am your teacher and you are Ramona'. And you can say 'I am Ramona and you are my teacher'. It's the way we all talk about ourselves.

I looked at the letter with new respect, this letter that allowed you to show what it was like to look out of this face, with these eyes at the big world. This was the letter to describe the me-ness of things. At that moment the world deepened for me. And reading was the tool with which I would begin to make sense of it.

I realised that reading was the key that opened the door to secret lands, strange places and the worlds behind other people's eyes. Much later, when I discovered the hidden promises of a toy microscope, I became aware of similar possibilities—of fantastic worlds revealed only through the lens. I had the same thrill when I discovered the night sky through a telescope on a school excursion to the planetarium. There were millions of stars beyond the ones we could see with our eyes, and beyond those too, a carpet of twinkling blackness opened up forever.

But, until I could master enough language to be able to read the kinds of things that interested me, I loved to be told stories.

One of the first I remember was told to me by my father who, like my mother, was a Jewish Holocaust survivor from Poland. Aaron was born in 1918, and became a tailor's apprentice at thirteen. His first job was to run between the blacksmith's forge and the tailor's shop, with hot coals for their irons. A few years later he was cutting out patterns and sewing men's three-piece suits, and what he called 'costumes' for women. He was short like my mother. His eyes were brown and his straight hair, which he used brylcreem to brush back without a part, was black.

So what did he think important to tell a child? A woodcutter was wandering about in a forest...

I imagined it was in Poland. I always thought Poland was cold and possibly snowy but when I went there it was summer and the cornflowers were blooming in the fields. Or perhaps they were rye flowers. I'm sure there must be rye flowers in Poland, although I'm not certain they are blue. And the flowers in Poland were blue.

Anyway, in this story, my father said, there is a man who then and there comes upon a bird that he wants to kill and carry home to feed his family. I remember my father saying that he grabs the bird, which I thought would be hard because they are such sensitive flighty things— none of those that I had chased in the St Kilda gardens would ever have been caught by grabbing. And maybe my father, the uneducated Polish tailor, didn't know the right English word.

But now the bird is in the man's hands. And just before he kills the bird—and, did I tell you, I am five years old when this killing is about to happen—before he breaks its neck, it speaks to him. 'Don't kill me,' says the bird. 'Why not?' says the man. 'Because if you let me live I will reward you by telling you three secrets of life.' 'All right,' says the man. 'What are they?' 'One—don't believe what you are told. Two—don't climb higher than you can. And three— don't reach for things beyond your grasp.' So the man lets the bird go and it flies and flies, higher and higher, onto the top of a tall tree. I imagined a Christmas tree, not a straggly gum tree or one of the palms on Beaconsfield Parade, across the road from our flat. And now the bird begins to laugh, and, really, I hear it as a cruel laugh, a jeering laugh. And I hear the voice of the bird, no longer sweet. 'Oh, you are such a stupid man! You let me go, but I have a heart that is pure and solid gold, and if you had killed me you would have had riches beyond your dreams. And now you have nothing! Not even a bird for your dinner!' This makes the man angry. He realises that he has lost his fortune. And he begins to climb the big tree. And he climbs it to the very top where the branches get smaller and smaller and hard to hold and sway in the wind. And just when he gets to the topmost branch and the bird is within his grasp, it takes flight and hovers above his head. He holds out his hand to reach it, loses his balance and topples over, crashing to the ground. He is dead. And, my father said, the man thought he had lost his fortune but, actually, he had been given three secrets of life. He was told not to believe what he was told, and yet he believed the bird had a golden heart. And he was told not to climb higher than he could and he didn't listen, and he climbed to the top of the tree. My father's voice reached a crescendo. And he was told not to reach for things beyond his grasp and he did, and he fell to his death.

What a strange story! But I liked it and I would ask my father to tell it again and again. I was intrigued by the paradox of being advised not to listen to advice. It was the opposite of romantic stories about heroic adventures and magic powers and brave quests. It grew out of a reality where no one expected too much and it was best not to disturb the order of things.

This was the world my father was born into. His mother was widowed with four children after his father came back from fighting World War One only to succumb to the flu in 1919. She rented an apple orchard and, each year, sold part of the crop, stored some fruit in the cellar for the winter, and paid the rest of the crop as rent to the owner, just as if it was the Middle Ages. When I began to work in broadcasting, my father said: If you have to speak up, speak nicely and, above all, don't be controversial. He never listened to my programs for fear he'd hear me say something that would worry him.

On the other side of our building in St Kilda, in the exact mirror-image flat to ours, lived Lillian and Tommy. I thought of them as an old couple but they were probably younger than I am now. My parents said Lillian was the daughter of a Jewish-English family, and she had come to Australia to marry Tom, an Aussie soldier returned from World War One.

Now a travelling salesman selling superphosphate to

farmers, Tom would go off on trips for weeks at a time. If he was days later than his promised return he would tell his wife that he had spent time on the Murray River fishing, but my father said that Tommy stopped at a fish and chip shop on the way home and bought the fish from there, in order to fool his wife.

As a matter of fact, almost everything I knew about them was from overhearing my parents talking, though I did wander over to Lillian and Tommy's flat some mornings. I would get into bed with Tommy who would be reading the *Sun*. He had his first beer of the day by his bedside and he'd teach me to read the 'funnies' as he called them—the comic strip with Dagwood and Blondie Bumstead. He called me Blondie too.

At primary school they played us a recording of Oscar Wilde's *The Happy Prince*. Another story about a bird and a man, but this time the man was a statue of a prince, and the bird was a swallow that had come to rest at his feet after a day of travelling. The swallow was on his way to Egypt to join his friends, after having waited behind to resolve an impossible love affair with an unsuitable object—a reed, in fact.

It was narrated with sonorous authority by Orson Welles, his serious precision chiming with the lighter, boyish sound of the young Bing Crosby as the prince.

I found the same recording while I was writing this

book, and heard again, fifty years later, Orson and Bing and the orchestral music that underscored the story, telling you what to feel. It took me back to St Kilda Park State School where we sat on the mat at story time.

'High above the city,' Orson begins, 'on a tall column, stood the statue of the Happy Prince. He was gilded all over with thin leaves of fine gold, for eyes he had two bright sapphires, and a large red ruby glowed on his sword-hilt.'

The story tells of the prince's awareness, after a life of carefree happiness, that there are people in his city who are poor and need help. His tears soak the little swallow as he shelters at the prince's feet.

'When I was alive and had a human heart,' he says, 'I did not know what tears were, for I lived in the palace of Sans-Souci, where sorrow is not allowed to enter...So I lived, and so I died. And now that I am dead they have set me up here so high that I can see all the ugliness and all the misery of my city, and though my heart is made of lead yet I cannot choose but weep.'

Can you imagine how sad this sounded to my five-year-old self?

The prince asks the swallow to help him, and slowly the sapphires and the ruby and the leaves of gold are plucked by the bird and given to the poor people of the city (including a writer in a garret who is trying to finish a play). But winter comes and the prince has given everything away and the swallow has missed his opportunity to fly to Egypt and he falls dead from the cold at the statue's feet. And somehow the statue is dead again, too, and he's melted down by the burghers of the city because he is no longer beautiful and the only thing left is his heart of lead.

And the story ends like this: ' "What a strange thing!" said the overseer of the workmen at the foundry. "This broken lead heart will not melt in the furnace. We must throw it away." So they threw it on a dust-heap where the dead swallow was also lying.'

Then Orson says, ' "Bring me the two most precious things in the city," said God to one of his angels; and the angel brought him the leaden heart and the dead bird.'

I adore this tale of sacrifice and love. After all this time, it still has the power to move me. How different is the sweet swallow from the nasty trickster in the Polish forest! But, again, there is a paradox—the prince enlists the swallow to bring happiness to people in the city, and in the process causes the death of the good little bird. So strongly had I been moved by the goodness of the creature, that I identified it closely to myself. It was only on rehearing the original recording that I realised the bird was male and not female, as I had first remembered.

There were other stories I found equally unforgettable. When I was nine, I read Hans Christian Andersen's story, *The Red Shoes*, about an orphan girl called Karen who wants a pair of red shoes like she has seen a princess wear. She manages to acquire a pair and not only wears them to church, already a show-offy thing to do, but—worse still—she thinks about them when she is taking communion.

Of course she has to be punished.

An old soldier with a red beard whom she passes outside the church casts a spell and that is it. She is cursed to dance uncontrollably until she meets an executioner. And she is so tired from the manic dancing that she begs him to cut off her feet, which he does, and her feet go on dancing in the red shoes around the countryside.

'And he carved her a pair of wooden feet and some crutches,' the story says, 'and taught her a psalm which is always sung by sinners; she kissed the hand that guided the axe, and went away over the heath.'

She goes on to become a very pious girl who is finally allowed back to church, minus her feet. I can still see the bloody feet in the red shoes dancing and dancing over the wooded landscape.

So never want what a princess has—but if you do happen to get it, don't think about it in church, or your feet will have to come off and you will have to kiss the hand of the man who chops them. Another paradox—the God of forgiveness and do-unto-others was so unreasonably cruel to a poor girl who was already an orphan, just because she loved her red shoes!

The stories I heard before I knew how to read were like a drug for me, but if childhood is a time of innocence, tales like these were an assault on grace.

I was introduced to the *Victorian Readers* later, which were used as class sets to teach reading. Here we learned to recite Banjo Paterson's 'Clancy of the Overflow', 'Bell-Birds' by Henry Kendall and 'My Country' by Dorothea Mackellar.

I vividly remember 'A Brave Australian Girl' in the Fourth Book, the real story of sixteen-year-old Grace Bussell who grew up on a farm near Cape Leeuwin in Western Australia, and rode a horse into dangerous waters to rescue passengers from the shipwrecked *Georgette* in 1876. She was called the 'Grace Darling of Australia'. The English Grace Darling, told of in Wordsworth's 1843 poem, was then introduced by the teacher. She had helped her father rescue the survivors of the 1838 shipwreck of the SS *Forfarshire*, off the coast where she lived:

> When, as day broke, the Maid, through misty air,
> Espies far off a Wreck, amid the surf,
> Beating on one of those disastrous isles—
> Half of a Vessel, half—no more; the rest
> Had vanished, swallowed up with all that there
> Had for the common safety striven in vain,

Or thither thronged for refuge. With quick glance
Daughter and Sire through optic-glass discern,
Clinging about the remnant of this Ship,
Creatures—how precious in the Maiden's sight!
For whom, belike, the old Man grieves still more
Than for their fellow-sufferers engulfed
Where every parting agony is hushed,
And hope and fear mix not in further strife.
'But courage, Father! let us out to sea—
A few may yet be saved.'

There seemed to me to be plenty of opportunities for brave rescues by plucky girls. The *Victorian Readers* were introduced to schoolchildren early in the twentieth century in order to teach us moral principles, pride in our British heritage and a terror of the bush. We were to be good and brave, helpful and studious.

The other memorable piece was 'The Drover's Wife' by Henry Lawson. The story in the Fifth Reader still touches me, of the woman alone, waiting for her husband who has not been home for six months, each Sunday taking the pram and the dog and other kids for a walk through the bush in her best clothes, though no one could possibly see her. She realises there is a snake under the house and she decamps with the children to the bark kitchen where she keeps a vigil all night. After the dog kills the snake:

She lays her hand on the dog's head, and all the fierce,

angry light dies out of his yellow eyes. The younger children are quieted, and presently go to sleep. The boy stands for a moment in his shirt, watching the fire. Presently he looks up at her, sees the tears in her eyes, and, throwing his arms around her neck exclaims:

'Mother, I won't never go drovin'.'

And she hugs him to her breast and kisses him; and they sit thus together while the sickly daylight breaks over bush.

Lawson, in fact, wrote, 'The dirty-legged boy stands for a moment in his shirt,' and the boy says, 'Mother, I won't never go drovin' blarst me if I do!' before 'she hugs him to her worn-out breast'. The vigilant editors of the *Readers* took the view that on their watch no fine Australian example of womanhood would be permitted to have worn-out breasts or to keep her son less than perfectly clean.

Even so, I have never forgotten the sickly daylight after the all-night vigil, an image of utter exhaustion. Both Lawson's and Wordsworth's texts, and the anonymous story of Grace Bussell are about female courage in the face of immense odds. And they contradicted my father's story of not reaching beyond your grasp, but I can only see that now. I must have doubted the wisdom of my father even then, and sought the stories that would tell me otherwise.

## CHAPTER 2

# Only as old as her feet

---

Ioffically lost my literary innocence on the floor of the Camberwell Mobile Library in 1965, when I was ten. We had moved from our rented flat across the road from the beach in St Kilda to a small three-bedroom solid brick house in North Balwyn, a respectable suburb with many churches and no pubs. We didn't mix with the neighbours much for the first few years, and I didn't realise until later that many of the houses in the street were of exactly the same design as ours. Even so, my parents were terribly proud to have been able to buy our house, and there were many conversations about our mortgage that would be revisited for years to come.

I'm not sure if they still have this kind of service in North Balwyn but the bus library used to come and park down near the shops.

For immigrant families like mine, where the parents were educated only to primary level and not in English, the bus was much less daunting than the big main library near the Camberwell Town Hall. Such institutions were hard to navigate when you looked different and spoke with an accent. There were fewer books on the bus, and the atmosphere was more intimate.

So Mama took my hand and got me registered, and I had a card of which I was as proud as my parents were of our house. I was shown which books were for children and which for grown-ups. But I quickly tired of the children's section. I discovered that, as I lay on my belly on the bus floor, with its smell of lino and rubber, deciding which books to take, I could read the spines in the adult section. There I spied Kafka and Kazantzakis, Kerouac and Koestler. There I learned to put things into alphabetical order.

I decided to sample Kafka's *The Trial* because, as you might remember, it's rather a slim volume. I took the book to the librarian who had a small desk and chair at the back of the bus, near the door.

'Please sir,' I said, like Oliver Twist, 'may I have this one?'

'But that's for adults,' he said. 'You're only in Grade Six.'

'But please, sir, I've read all the interesting ones for kids. I'd really like to try this. It's only small.'

And he let me borrow it.

I walked home gravely, the book in my clammy hand, its plastic covering getting misty.

Actually I hadn't read all the books for kids—C. S. Lewis had passed me by, and so had Tolkien. Kenneth Grahame's *The Wind in the Willows* was as foreign as the English countryside it depicted. Thinking back now, it's entirely possible that they were not represented in the bus library's collection, but it's more likely that I had no truck with talking animals. But the attitude of the bus librarian gave me confidence, and the bus itself was small enough to make me think I had its measure and that people in there would take me seriously. In his 1947 report, 'Public Libraries in Australia', Lionel McColvin said of these kinds of services, 'Nowhere else in the English-speaking world will books have to be taken so far for so few, and nowhere else will they mean so much.'

Later I found a book that has haunted me for years— *Hills End* by Australian writer Ivan Southall. Many children read this book at school in the mid-sixties and it's regarded as a turning point in Australian children's literature. It marked the beginning of a series of novels in which Southall tackled the idea of children surviving terrible events.

The story follows seven children and their teacher who are trapped inside a cave while a fierce cyclonic storm

destroys the fictional town of Hills End. They face a strug-
gle to survive as well as having to deal with their loss. It
was about survival of the spirit as much as survival of the
species.

I wondered how I would fare if my parents were killed.
I knew that their parents and families had been killed in
the Holocaust and they were both the only survivors. Each
had a complex story. My mother had survived the war by
taking another identity, and had been alone from the age
of fourteen, and my father had hidden in a cellar for two
years. That was all I knew. They cried whenever I asked
them to tell me of their experiences, and I learned that my
questions were upsetting and not welcome so I stopped asking. It was better to read and to imagine. *Hills End* chimed
with me and allowed me to imagine the details that I never
really learned from them.

Once, when I was about eight, my father came home
after one of the annual gatherings of survivors that com-
memorated the Holocaust, with a glossy magazine of
photographs from Auschwitz. Without any warning, he
handed it to me. The gold Hebrew lettering on the cover
attracted my eye, but over the page there were horrible
photographs of piles of dead naked people, and when I
turned to the next page to expunge the image, it gave way
to another, more terrible photograph of thin children sitting up on trays before they were to go into ovens. That's

what I remember seeing. It was shocking. I don't want to find a digital version of the image again in order to check my memory, even for you.

My mama grabbed the magazine from my hands when she realised what it was, screaming at my father that I was too young to see such things. They had a huge argument, all in Polish, swearing at each other. I lost my appetite for dinner. We were having barley soup, and for years afterwards the smell of it made me sick. Once, during my regular rifling of my parents' wardrobe and drawers, I found the book high on a shelf. I recognised the cover and didn't have to open it. I was scared of that wardrobe, and avoided it for years afterwards. I developed a strange tic of making sure all wardrobe doors in any room I ever slept in were closed before I could go to sleep.

Perhaps my mother forbade books about the war after that, because it was only while visiting other people's houses as a teenager that I saw books such as *House of Dolls* by Yehiel De-Nur, whose pen name was Ka-Tsetnik 135633, derived from his Auschwitz prisoner number. It was about Jewish women serving in concentration camp brothels, but I did not read it. I flicked through it and got the general idea.

I read *The Diary of a Young Girl* by Anne Frank as my high school years began, but remember being more interested in the crush that grew between Anne and Peter as they spent month after month together in the attic, keeping their voices low, than in the politics of the Dutch resistance to the Nazis, and Anne's death in Bergen-Belsen. Survival stories were common in our circle, but love stories were hard to come by.

The bus library introduced me to a different world and I'm sure that's why Mama took me there. I've had conversations over the years with some of the best writers on the planet, and when they speak about their introduction to reading, which nearly always determines their impulse to write, many will talk of a local library or librarian or a kind teacher as the source of their life-long love of books.

For English novelist Jeanette Winterson, whose adoptive parents were fundamentalist Christians who owned only six books, all of them about the Bible, books from the library were her path to the outside world. But everything she brought home from the library was vetted by her mother, and young Jeanette began to hide books under her bed. She was caught with a copy of *Women in Love*, and her mother knew enough to know that D. H. Lawrence was a satanist and a pornographer.

Her mother threw all the books out of her bedroom window and set fire to them in the backyard in front of the outside toilet.

'I often think', Jeanette told me, 'that the reason why tyrants hate books, and how they do book-burning sessions regularly and book-banning, is not so much what the books contain…[but] because reading itself is an act of free will. Nothing can come between you and a book—there's no surveillance camera, there's no little bugging device from the CIA that can get into that space between your mind and the page—so it's terrifying. And it does mean independence of mind and spirit; nobody knows what you're thinking at that time.'

My mother was completely different from Mrs Winterson. She read widely in popular non-fiction—Alvin Toffler's *The Third Wave*, Vance Packard's *The Hidden Persuaders* and *The Waste Makers*. She read political books and feminist books. Most of all she adored books that had been banned. She read James Joyce's *Ulysses*, which was banned in Australia till 1953. I can't imagine what she made of it, since English was a foreign language for her; I had trouble reading it in my mother tongue. She read D. H. Lawrence's *Lady Chatterley's Lover*, banned until 1965, Philip Roth's *Portnoy's Complaint*, unbanned in 1970 after a massive court case and an illegal Australian printing. These books were all part of her reveries on her reading couch.

By the time she bought them it was perfectly legal to do so, but I didn't know that at the time, and I sometimes wondered if the Vice Squad was about to knock on our door. My mama didn't keep them from me, but as I was completely innocent of anything to do with sex I had trouble working out exactly what the incendiary passages were. I remember thinking that some nude swimming in *Ulysses* must have been the problem, completely missing what Molly Bloom was talking about in her soliloquy. By the time Henry Miller's *Tropic of Cancer* was unbanned in 1973 I was already at university. I found it strangely arousing and searched out his *Tropic of Capricorn* for more of the same. Up until then Miller had been the author with the most books banned in Australia.

I once asked my mother to buy a book for me that I had heard about—how I can't remember—because I had the impression that it was very interesting. She wrote down the title in her slow hand on an envelope and took it into the city with her so she could buy it after her doctor's appointment.

When she got home Mama described how she passed the note over to the bookseller. 'My daughter wants me to get this,' she told him.

The bookseller became flustered. 'How old is your daughter?' he asked.

'Twelve,' she replied.

Nonetheless my mother bought the book and in the tram on the way home she took it out of its paper bag and opened it up. She reported to us that the man sitting opposite her seemed surprised to see a middle-aged woman

reading the *Kama Sutra* on the number 48 to North
Balwyn.

After she got used to the flowery language of the ancient Indian Sanscrit sex manual written by Vatsyayana
and translated by Sir Richard Burton, my dear mother was
not fooled by the confusing categories of the hare man, the
bull man, and the horse man, according to the size of his
lingam, and, according to the depth of her yoni, the female
categories of the deer, the mare, or the female elephant.
She knew what was what and realised that the chapters
devoted to types of embraces and kissing, and different
kinds of marks to be made by nails and teeth, were all
possibly questionable as a subject for the twelve-year-old
mind. When I came home from school there was a minor
Spanish Inquisition to check if I had any idea of what the
book was about, and a marginally heightened exposition
on how embarrassed she had been, but to her credit my
mother let me take the *Kama Sutra* into my room to try
and make sense of it.

Which was not easy, especially the puzzling chapter
on women who stand in doorways or who are always looking out into the street—these were among the women who
were the most easily seduced. Was this manual a relic of
another time and place, or were these truths universally
held? How could I know? My mama wasn't telling either.
But I learned that:

> A woman who hears a man playing on a reed
> pipe which has been dressed with the juices of the
> bahupadika plant, the tabernamontana coronaria, the
> costus speciosus or arabicus, the pinus deodora, the
> euphorbia antiquorum, the vajra and the kantaka plant,
> becomes his slave.

And:

> If the bone of a camel is dipped into the juice of the
> plant eclipta prostata, and then burnt, and the black
> pigment produced from its ashes is placed in a box also
> made of the bone of a camel, and applied together with
> antimony to the eye lashes with a pencil also made of
> the bone of a camel, then that pigment is said to be very
> pure, and wholesome for the eyes, and serves as a means
> of subjugating others to the person who uses it.

How to get hold of camel bones and dressed reed pipes?
Love was a complex and mysterious art but I was about to
find another source of instruction.

My parents were always trying one way or another to
get ahead and make some extra cash. They were not good
at it.

One year they took another smaller mortgage and
bought a large run-down boarding house. They spent their
weekends off from their factory jobs cleaning the corridors
and the public rooms of the place and collecting the rent.
One weekend my father was agitated to find that a couple

had done a flit, leaving rent several months in arrears and their room in a mess. He salvaged a three-legged occasional table and a book that I have on my shelf to this day.

*Home Management: Volume 1* was edited by Alison Barnes and published by George Newnes Limited of London. It's undated but I believe it came out early in the 1950s, using illustrations and photos from decades before.

Confidently it told me all about the perfect family in the perfect home, how to make sure you have one and how to keep it humming. 'The housewife's best weapon against moth and other pests is a spray gun of DDT used generously and often,' it advises under a photograph of a woman with a bobbed dark helmet of hair, an impossibly white apron and sleek high heels, wielding said gun.

From making old scraps from the larder really appetising ('diced cold meat takes on a new lease of life set in aspic jelly with a few peas and egg slices for colour') to planning a funeral ('if, for any reason, a disinterment is necessary, permission must first be given from the Home Office'), the book has everything. But it was the section on Sex Education that I was driven to after the *Kama Sutra*. It made no mention of exotic animals or the practices of courtesans, but advised that, 'Adolescents should be taught that sexual desire is normal, that no harm can come from continence, and that it is advisable to engage actively in recreational pastimes, while trying to avoid consciously thinking about sex.' I was disturbed by learning that 'children from unhappy homes seldom make happy marriages when they become men and women' and that 'no human instinct is more liable to distortion in early life than the sexual instinct'.

But then I happily found that 'a woman is only as old as her feet' and that 'a goat will quickly learn to jump up on to a bench about 14 inches high, which makes milking more comfortable for both'. I saw how to lay out a herbaceous border, and discovered a recipe for nettle beer. Duck-keeping for profit sat beside an article on growing your own smokes—and blending the tobacco to suit your own personal tastes. As one who is always on the lookout for massive catastrophes, I have hung on to *Home Management* with its arcane but handy hints despite several house moves and many book-culls.

I sometimes wonder why it was abandoned in that crummy boarding house. Maybe it had been a wedding present to a hopeful blushing bride, and the room she found herself in fell far short of the perfect home in the perfect dream. No lily pond with arbour, no pantry, no training everyone to 'use a clothes brush morning and night on outer garments of all but the finest fabrics' and helping the drill 'by keeping good brushes at all strategic points'. *Home Management* came to me on a wave of irony long before I developed an appreciation of the form.

But, as has been the case all my life, whenever I had a question, or even before I could formulate one, the right book arrived to offer answers. I had begun to discover that books could provide all kinds of confusing information about sex. Now I was about to learn what books could teach their readers about love.

## CHAPTER 3

# *The ferocity of love*

---

While Mama read her way through banned books, and books about social and political change, I was becoming a dutiful student of literature, and worked my way through the reading lists for my year levels at high school.

I studied *The Red Badge of Courage* by Stephen Crane, his 1895 American Civil War story of bravery, cowardice and the making of men, *Rogue Male* by Geoffrey Household, the 1939 thriller set in the wilds of the English countryside, *Catcher in the Rye* by J. D. Salinger, and other books too. Nothing, however, spoke to me in such a monumental way as a small book of two collections of stories, *My Mother's House* and *Sido*, by a French writer with just one name—Colette.

I think I was enticed by the point of view of the young child who had been christened Sidonie-Gabrielle Colette, as she remembered her childhood house in the village of Saint-Sauveur. Colette lived with her mother, Sido, and her father, Jules-Joseph Colette, her mother's older, gruff second husband, who had lost a leg fighting the Austrians at Melegnano, in the Second Italian War of Independence. He was passionately in love with Sido. She called him 'the Captain'; the children—Colette and her older brother Leo (who was conceived when Sido was still married to her violent, drunken first husband), as well as the two children of her first marriage, Achille and Juliette—were 'the savages'.

In this book, surrounded by the sensuality of her home and garden under Sido's care, and affectionately called Minet-Chéri by her mother, Colette tries to fathom everything she can about the adult world.

Throughout her life Colette was aware that her beloved mother had dominated much of her work:

Any writer whose existence is long drawn out turns in the end towards his past, either to revile it or rejoice in it. As a child I was poor but happy, like many children who need neither money nor comfort to achieve an active sort of happiness. But my felicity knew another and less commonplace secret: the presence of her who, instead of receding far from me through the gates of death, has revealed herself more vividly to me as I grow older...I am not at all sure that I have put the finishing touches to these portraits of her, nor am I at all sure that I have discovered all that she has bequeathed to me. I have come late to this task. But where could I find a better one for my last?

Our home was nothing like Colette's. Sido was always stopping in the garden to 'crack a dry poppy head with her finger-nail, rub the greenfly from a rose shoot, fill her pockets with unripe walnuts', but my mother had come from a farming family in the Polish countryside, and sometimes when we drove out into the hills on a Sunday she remarked on the richness of the soil or the smell of the air.

Sido was also a study in grown womanhood for Colette, as was my mama for me, although my mother was far more silent and mysterious. Perhaps in my thoughts about Colette and Sido I was trying to project myself into my mama's country childhood and imagine my grandmother, Rivka, after whom I was given my Hebrew name. Ramona was a name my mother had heard in a song on the radio when she was pregnant. 'Ramona, I hear the mission bells above / Ramona, they're ringing out our song of love.' She thought it was safer to name me something not immediately identifiable as Jewish. Just in case.

Why else would a young girl relate so strongly to the wistfulness of the first story in *My Mother's House*?

To Colette describing Sido calling into the garden over and over:

> Where are the children?
> Two are at rest. The others grow older day by day.
> If there be a place of waiting after this life, then surely
> she who so often waited for us has not ceased to
> tremble for those two who are yet alive.

My mother's father died when she was two months old. At fourteen, in 1942, she was sent by her mother to Warsaw, where the family knew people who would arrange forged identity papers. From this time, she was on her own. After the war Mama discovered the rest of her family had been murdered. I imagined her mother, Rivka, as Sido, waiting for her and worrying about her in an afterlife.

I have just re-read the chapter in *My Mother's House* called 'Jealousy'. It summons another memory. Sido is off to the butcher to buy meat for their dinner, still in her apron, while her husband fusses and glares as he looks at his watch, waiting for her return. When she does he accuses her of dallying with a view to making eyes at the young men in town:

> Indignantly my mother folds her hands, pretty still
> though ageing and weather-beaten, over a bosom held
> up by gusseted stays. Blushing beneath the bands of her
> greying hair, her chin trembling with resentment, this

little elderly lady is charming when she defends herself
without so much as a smile against the accusations of
a jealous sexagenarian. Nor does he smile either, as he
goes on to accuse her now of 'gallivanting'. But I can
still smile at their quarrels because I am only fifteen,
and have not yet divined the ferocity of love beneath his
veteran eyebrow, and the blushes of adolescence upon
her fading cheeks.

It was the last sentence I puzzled over. The ferocity of his
love and the blushes of adolescence upon her fading cheeks
were completely unfamiliar to my fifteen-year-old self, not
because I could not respond to such things at that tender
age, but because I knew there was no such passion in my
home. So it was like that, the passion between a man and
his wife, that does not fade, that survives the years of do-
mesticity and the missteps of living?

My parents didn't talk about how they met or why they
were together. They fought about money and didn't seem
to have anything in common. Years after my mother had
died and I was planning a trip to Poland to make a radio
documentary, I asked my father to explain where in his
birthplace town of Siedlce they had met, and subsequently
married. He told me that in 1945 he had been helping
with a survey of the surviving Jews in the town. When the
Russian army had liberated Warsaw, my mother had gone
east to her village to find her family. Having learned they

had all been killed, some by villagers and the rest at the death camp of Treblinka, she tried to kill herself. She was taken to hospital in Siedlce to recover.

When she was released two months later, the war was over. She was sitting, as she had told me once, 'in the gutter', when my father came by and asked if she was Jewish. She was seventeen. He was nine years older. She said, 'I sold myself to him for a stale roll and half a pint of milk.'

But he told a different story. He said that when she found out that he had a book in his digs, she started to visit him. The book was *Quo Vadis: A Narrative of the Time of Nero* by the Polish writer and Nobel Prize winner Henryk Sienkiewicz, a historical novel of which she never spoke. I wondered why she had never told me about the book. I sought it out when I remembered my father's story.

As I read the opening chapters I imagined Mama at seventeen, alone, war-ravaged, just out of hospital and absorbed by this story of devoted love between the beautiful Christian convert Lygia and the young patrician and tribune Marcus Vinicius. He rescues her from death in the Coliseum, and becomes a convert too. I was puzzled about why this book would be a driver for Mama to connect with my father and seek him out. *Quo Vadis* was a classic of Polish literature, but in her orthodox family secular works would not have been encouraged. And she had left school in the sixth grade, when she was eleven, so she would not have read it there.

I knew that she had spent six months learning to pass herself off as a devout Catholic at the house of the people who arranged her false identity papers, memorising the prayers by heart, and getting used to kneeling on stone floors. She told me that the son-in-law of the owner of the house lived with them. He was a journalist, so there must have been books to read. Perhaps she had already started reading *Quo Vadis*. When the journalist found out that they were harbouring a young Jewess, he insisted she leave, as it was becoming too dangerous for his family. Perhaps meeting my father and seeing the book again, she was held in its thrall. Did it connect her to a time when she thought her family was alive, and there was still hope?

All my ideas on this are pure conjecture now, but if she thought my father would rescue her, like Marcus Vinicius, she was mistaken. He could not even rescue himself. They were two needy souls with nothing but sadness to give to one another.

I wonder at her sense of romance. How could it have survived all the things she had seen? Was she thirsty to learn about love from books too?

In a chapter of *My Mother's House* called 'My Mother and the Books' Colette herself learns that love is 'complicated, tyrannical and even burdensome' and that Sido was sceptical about it:

'It's a great bore—all the love in these books,' she used to say. 'In life, my poor Minet-Chéri, folk have other fish to fry. Did none of these lovesick people you read of have children to rear or a garden to care for? Judge for yourself, Minet-Chéri, have you or your brothers ever heard me harp on love as they do in books?'

But books were exactly where children like me looked for instruction about love and how families worked, or more to the point how other people's families—normal families, happy families—worked. I kept an eye on the people across the road, for example, who had four children and were Catholic. Every Friday night the father would get off the tram from the city (he worked in the tax office) carrying home a great big parcel of fried fish and chips and potato cakes.

We could see him wearing his hat with the warm parcel under one arm and holding a bouquet of flowers for his wife in the other hand. Unlike my parents, the tax official and his wife slept in the same bed, but my mother once told me that his wife didn't like to have sex with him. She had told my mother, 'He knows he can have it if he really needs to,' which sounded rather begrudging, even to me, who knew nothing at all of such things.

And while my mother indicated that fish and chips and flowers may not tell you much about what is really happening in a marriage, she didn't give away any clues about how a happy marriage might work. At fourteen I wanted to go to a dance at the local town hall, and she forbade me. When I said I'd never fall in love if I never met anyone, she said I'd only need to meet one person and that when I fell in love I'd know it. I shouted at her, 'What would you know about love?' and she hit me with such ferocity that I had a big black eye by the morning. She said to say that a cricket ball hit me, if anyone asked about it at school. I was no wiser about happy marriages.

Colette wrote about all kinds of love—between women, between young people, between husbands and wives, between older women and young men. Later I read *Cheri* and *Claudine at School* and *The Vagabond*. She used her experiences in the demi-monde of the theatre and the literary salons to make some very quotable statements that I suspected were the kinds of things my mother might know if she were inclined to tell.

For instance: 'You will do foolish things, but do them with enthusiasm.' And: 'If I can't have too many truffles, I'll do without truffles.'

Mama did quote a Yiddish proverb once: *Az me est chazzer, zol rinnen fun bord.* Literally, if you're going to eat pork, make sure it drips on your beard, or, if you're going to be bad, make sure you enjoy it.

There is a photograph of Colette, taken on her

eightieth birthday in 1953 by Walter Carone, in which she sits up in what could be her bed, and on a table shelf in front of her the candles on her beautiful creamy torte light up and burst into flames, as if all the brandy in the cake has ignited at once. It captures a moment of dangerous excess, and represents all the mysterious and succulent elements of my Colette phase.

But while I delighted in and even envied the garden and the passions that Colette wrote about in those first stories, nothing surprised and affected me more than another book I read at school, *The Man who Loved Children* by Christina Stead.

Until then, all the families in the books I had read were happy, or at least they were not riven with fault lines and historical tragedies like mine was. I never saw one skerrick of affection between my parents, not a kiss, not a touch. Every day we would steel ourselves for meal time, when, at best, sarcasm would be served with dinner, at worst, shouting and swearing in Polish.

But the complexities of the Pollit family (Sam and his second wife Henny, his fourteen-year-old daughter from his first marriage, Louisa, and the six little ones from his second marriage), the chasms between what Louisa imagined and her reality, helped me understand that the unhappiness of my family was not an experience I was having on my own. A writer was allowed to write about unhappy family life and I was allowed to read about it too.

Sam Pollit is a cruel, brilliant and narcissistic scientist who uses words as weapons to wield power over his exhausted wife and their children, especially Louisa, who falls short of his standards of beauty and grace. The keen eye of Stead, as given to Louisa, was proof that a child/woman could correctly evaluate a situation and make a fair critique of the actions and motivations of her parents. She could be right and the parents could be so wrong. It was revolutionary. And liberating, though my family life was nothing like Louisa's. And, despite the novel's Baltimore setting, I knew it had been written by an Australian woman. It felt close to home.

My French teacher set *Madame Bovary* for us (in English) and at the age of sixteen I dipped my toe into the world according to Gustave Flaubert. Emma Bovary, like Henny, is another unhappily married woman but she tries to solve her need for romance through adultery. Her rebellion against the expectations of her provincial surrounds leads to her downfall, and that of her child. I wrote an essay on the novel and called Emma 'a woman ahead of her time', paraphrasing my mama, who had read the book in French. I was the only one in the class who didn't think Madame Bovary was a bad mother and wife, only that she was a disappointed and bored woman.

Before her marriage, she had believed that what she was experiencing was love; but since the happiness that should have resulted from that love had not come, she thought she must have been mistaken. And Emma tried to find out just what was meant, in life, by the words 'bliss', 'passion', and 'intoxication', which had seemed so beautiful to her in books.

Reading about the fictional lives of Emma Bovary and Henny Pollit and observing my own Mama's life I could see that the road was not necessarily happy for women, no matter where they lived or even when.

I re-read *Madame Bovary* recently and was surprised by the way the story begins, with the description of Charles Bovary, Emma's husband, as a new boy in a classroom of mean children, and his unwaveringly contained responses to their taunts. I realised that Flaubert wanted us to see things from Charles' point of view too, and that Emma's unhappiness was a sadness for him.

It was disconcerting for the novel to seem so different when I re-read it. Of course we are a different person each time we open a book to read it again; we can never really experience it in the same way, just as we can never step into the same stream twice.

This time, reading *Madame Bovary* from the vantage point of age and experience, I was aware that my life of reading had attuned me to all of the things that

Flaubert wanted me to understand by the way he told his story. And yet, partly because she reminded me of my mama, with her disappointments and her head always in a book, I willed myself as an adolescent to understand Emma Bovary.

> Deep in her soul, however, she was waiting for something to happen. Like a sailor in distress, she would gaze out over the solitude of her life with desperate eyes, seeking some white sail in the mists of the far-off horizon. She did not know what this chance event would be, what wind would drive it to her, what shore it would carry her to, whether it was a longboat or a three-decked vessel, loaded with anguish or filled with happiness up to the portholes. But each morning, when she awoke, she hoped it would arrive that day, and she would listen to every sound, spring to her feet, feel surprised that it did not come; then, at sunset, always more sorrowful, she would wish the next day were already there.

But Emma was also describing my own adolescent life. My mama guarded my social life and even shopped for my clothes. I was waiting for my own longboat or three-decked vessel to take me away. I imagined all kinds of futures for myself, as a noble and clever and virtuous woman making the world better. I assumed I'd have the love of my perfect man, who would be gifted and courageous. If my mother ever let me meet anyone. But, to her credit, Mama never restricted my reading life, and I was free to think about whatever I wanted, and imagine whatever story came to mind.

## CHAPTER 4

# Between knowing and telling

How strange then, armed as I was with all this knowledge of what might happen if a girl with too much of an interest in books marries the wrong man, I found myself married and pregnant at twenty to a young doctor, my own version of Charles Bovary. I had read the books that people had been reading that first year of university in the early seventies—*One Hundred Years of Solitude* by Gabriel García Márquez, *The Prophet* by Khalil Gibran, *Siddhartha* by Hermann Hesse, but I was deeply immersed by then in a science degree, and the warnings of Emma Bovary and the enticements of Colette were not at the front of my mind.

The truth was that, during all those afternoons of repose on the couch, my mama's reading under her blanket had masked her slow descent into illness. In my third year of university, she was diagnosed with chronic myeloid leukaemia, and there was no cure. My urgent impulse was to marry my boyfriend and present her with a grandchild, a naive defence against the inevitable. How could she die when there was a baby coming?

In my honours year in microbiology, I went into labour at the age of twenty-one and two weeks. I must have been completely ignorant of what exactly was going to happen to me since I packed my thesis so I could write between the contractions and finish it between the feeds. My friend Sally, seven years older and a single mother of a seven-year-old boy, explained that short stories were all that new mothers ever got a chance to finish. She gave me a collection called *The Little Disturbances of Man* by the Jewish-American writer Grace Paley. Paley's family had arrived from Ukraine at the beginning of the twentieth century, and she was a first-generation American gal, born in the Bronx, in New York. Her voice, formed in a family that spoke Russian and Yiddish, immediately resonated with me, making me laugh and cry. Her words seemed full of practical wisdom.

'Goodbye and Good Luck' is still my favourite, Paley's first story. She wrote it in 1956, at the age of thirty-four, and it's about an ageing woman reminiscing fondly about her youth and the love of her life (a womanising actor in the Yiddish theatre). It is a story we expect will end badly for her but, instead, it moves to an unexpectedly blissful conclusion. It begins like this:

> I was popular in certain circles, says Aunt Rose. I wasn't no thinner then, only more stationary in the flesh. In time to come, Lillie, don't be surprised—change is a fact of God. From this no one is excused. Only a person like your mama stands on one foot, she don't notice how big her behind is getting and sings in the canary's ear for thirty years…she waits in a spotless kitchen for a kind word and thinks—poor Rosie…
>
> Poor Rosie! If there was more life in my little sister, she would know my heart is a regular college of feelings and there is such information between my corset and me that her whole married life is a kindergarten.

I really want to read you the whole story—it is so lovely, so full of hope and grace. American novelist and critic Joyce Carol Oates said, 'How aptly named: Grace Paley. For "grace" is perhaps the most accurate, if somewhat poetic, term to employ in speaking of this gifted writer.' And, speaking of this first book, Oates added that Paley 'immediately drew an audience of readers who were not only admiring but loving'. And that she was a lyricist of the domestic life, writing of men and women, of children and parents and of politics. Paley was not a prolific writer. When asked why, she said, 'For me there is a lot of time between knowing and telling.' But why didn't she attempt longer, more ambitious and technically challenging fiction? 'Art is too long,' she said, 'and life is too short. There's a lot more to do in life than just writing.'

'I was a woman', Paley said on another occasion, 'writing at the early moment when small drops of worried resentment and noble rage were secretly, slowly building into the second wave of the women's movement. I didn't know my small-drop presence or usefulness in this accumulation.'

Grace Paley was seventy-eight when I finally met her in New York in 2001, at the French Roast, a coffee shop on the corner of 11th Street and 6th Avenue. She was tiny and I towered over her to kiss her hello. She had a beautiful open face, with high cheekbones and widely spaced eyes. Her hair was unruly, curly like mine. It had been fair, but now it was grey. She was five years older than my mother would have been. But mama died at forty-nine years of age so it was hard to imagine her as an old lady in my mind's eye.

Later Grace would tell me about a friend of hers who had died.

'Not like me,' she said, 'my friend was petite.'

'And you're not?' I asked, laughing.

'Petite in the garment industry but not in real life,' she said. 'I'm just short and fat.'

We sat in the corner of the café, eating salad and drinking coffee, and talking about the new president (the 'American coup', she called it), the Russians, the stories of Isaac Babel, our daughters, her grandchildren, adoption, women who had given up their babies, and her trip to Arizona to an Indian reservation for a writers' workshop.

She asked me to walk with her. She needed to do some shopping and offered to show me her neighbourhood.

'You know something about life?' she said, as we stood up from the table.

'Tell me,' I said.

'When you're seventy-eight and you get up from sitting at a table for a long time, your joints hurt.'

The reason we couldn't meet at her house, she said, was that her daughter Nora was not feeling well and had flown in from Vermont for a rest. Nora made her mother promise that she could have the house to herself.

'How old is your daughter?' I asked.

'She's a middle-aged woman. If she were younger, I'd know more how to handle her.'

She said her children resented her sociability when they were growing up. The number of people dropping by the house all the time bothered them, and now, she thought, maybe she had overdone it.

I was reminded of a story she had written called 'The Long Distance Runner':

Near home, I ran through our park, where I had aired
my children on weekends and late-summer afternoons.
I stopped at the north-east playground, where I met a
dozen young mothers intelligently handling their
little ones. In order to prepare them, meaning no
harm, I said, in fifteen years, you girls will be like me,
wrong in everything.

We walked past her house on 11th Street and she pointed
out the landmarks: the church, which was now a library,
and the women's prison, now a courtyard.

'Is that where you were kept when you got arrested
for your anti-nuclear protest?' I asked. It was. She wrote
a story about her character and alter ego, Faith, who had
been arrested at a demonstration. Her cell was full of black
women who were in for drugs, or violence, or prostitution.
When Faith explains why she's there, I vividly remember
one of them shouting to the guards, 'Get this housewife
outta here!'

We went to a hardware store to find some handles for
an old chest of drawers. I asked, as we walked along the
street, 'How is it when your friends die?'

'Terrible,' she said, 'and they go in batches.'

We talked about the merits of having younger or older
husbands. She said that friends who married younger men
were always concerned that their husbands would leave
them, especially as they got older.

'They always think it's the age,' she said, 'but it could be other things. I like my old man.'

She stopped for a moment and smiled to me as she talked of her husband, Robert, who at eighty-two had started a new publishing venture with her in order to 'publish books that lots of publishers have rejected'.

'I like my old man but I wouldn't want to be a younger woman married to an old man.'

She kept pausing in the street to tell me things about life. 'I had breast cancer last year. I had one breast removed but I'm fine now. I'm good.'

As we parted we saw a professional dog-walker with five charges. He tied them to a fire hydrant and went into a shop. They all sniffed each other's hindquarters and pissed on the hydrant. They looked just like a cartoon from the *New Yorker*.

She showed me the way home, we kissed, and she walked slowly back to 11th Street, her bushy grey hair blowing in the February wind.

As I watched her walking away, I thought that I could have been in a story by Paley. In many of them, the women simply go for long walks and talk. That day I had been given words of wisdom: a door had opened into her life and closed again as she walked away. I wished Mama had lived long enough to allow her to tell me things directly, like Grace did. But I suspect her secrecy was born of the years in which she acted a part to save her life, and couldn't be tempered by simply growing older. I hoped to be a wise and clear old lady like Grace.

She died in 2007 at the age of eighty-four. Jess Row wrote an obituary in *Slate*: 'Like all the greatest masters of the short story—Chekhov, Hemingway, Sholom Aleichem, Raymond Carver, Amy Hempel—Paley had an uncanny genius for containing a world within a sentence... Her stories are often described as having a spontaneous, performative quality, like dramatic monologues. But this is a carefully cultivated illusion—her language mimics colloquial speech but pares it down to nubbins of almost Beckett-like brevity.'

Not only does art imitate life but life imitates art. Perhaps we not only learn about life from stories, perhaps we make our lives through the stories we tell ourselves about the things that happen to us.

We read to find out what the world is like, to experience lots of lives, not just the one that we live. If it is true that our lives are chaotic and we crave a shape, stories are the shapes that we put on experience, containing all the wisdom in the world. We can even choose what kind of wisdom suits us.

'When people get old,' Paley told the *Paris Review* in 1994, 'they seem wise but it's only because they've got a little more experience, that's all. I'm not so wise. Two things happen when you get older. You have more experience, so you either seem wiser, or you get totally foolish. There are only those two options. You choose one, probably the wrong one.'

Paley was petite in the garment industry but not in real life. In reality, she was a giant. I can't walk with Paley in Greenwich Village any more but I can open her books and feel her there again, her hand on my hand, her smile across the table, her voice—or a voice like hers—saying, as she does in the opening line of one of her stories, 'There were two husbands disappointed by eggs...'

How could you do anything except see what happens next?

When my mama died I was pregnant with my younger daughter. It was a bleak year as I cared for my younger sister, my two-year-old toddler and my mother at home until three days before she died. Both that year and the year after, when my second daughter was born, there wasn't much time for reading. The days seemed grey and long, and I don't even remember a spring or summer.

But I did continue my interest in stories, and discovered Isaac Bashevis Singer. He won the Nobel Prize for literature in 1978, the year of my second daughter's birth, and new editions of his work were being published. His stories were precious for me as many of them were set in Jewish Poland before the war, and I thought they were a way for me to hold on to the connection with my mama, so cruelly severed by her death.

The town of Frampol and its environs, where many of his stories are set, was a community of rabbis and shoemakers, of farmers and shop owners, of passions and cruelties and love and sacrifice. But this world had another side where imps and dybbuks, ghosts and devils, witches and fallen angels all conspired to meddle with the souls of the inhabitants.

So even though I am immensely rational, I liked reading about the traps that the nether world set to test the purity and goodness of the characters, and it reminded me of the stories my mama would tell me about growing up in a family in which there were rules for every moment of the day—what you ate, what you wore, how you conducted yourself—and where there was superstition too. Whenever anyone told her what lovely daughters she had, she'd spit three times to avert the 'evil eye' and when she sewed a button on a shirt while we were wearing it, she made us hold a thread of red cotton in our mouths for the same reason.

But Singer's stories and novels were also full of desire and longing and sex and forbidden relationships and broken taboos. Of fools who triumph over those who jeer at them, of young women, like Yentl in his story 'Yentl the Yeshiva Boy' from *The Collected Stories*, whose desire to study the Talmud and whose aversion to the drudgeries of a woman's lot make her disguise herself as a young man called Anshel and go off to study in another town. In the study group, Anshel makes a wonderful friend of Avigdor, a young man who is in love with Hadass but unable to marry her, and the two 'men' fall in love without either of them being able to name the feelings. Anshel even marries Hadass, and manages to blood the sheets on the wedding night, and Hadass, the virgin, seems not to notice that Anshel is a girl. When Yentl finally shows Avigdor that she is a woman, she arranges to divorce Hadass who then is free to marry Avigdor, and the newly married couple name their first child Anshel, to the mystification of the local townsfolk.

The story is operatic in its mistaken identities, but again it speaks of the lengths to which clever girls might go to have a life of their own choosing.

It's a tradition, when a Jewish person dies, to light a candle that will burn for twenty-four hours, and to say a prayer for the dead. Isaac Bashevis Singer died at the age of eighty-eight in 1991. That night I lit a candle in the lounge room, on a bookshelf that held copies of his books. It was winter, and I went to bed thinking of his tales of passion and mysteries and ghosts.

In the middle of the night I heard glass smashing and voices calling and at first I thought I was dreaming, but when I went to the window of my room I saw flames pouring out of the house next door, a few feet away from me across the shared driveway.

As I stood in the street, with my children and our neighbours, all in our dressing gowns, watching the fire brigade fight in vain to save the house, I thought of my candle still flickering on my bookshelf, as the smoke rose from the burning roof across the way, a story befitting the great master storyteller himself.

## CHAPTER 5

# *What the guilty always say*

When the Camberwell bus librarian stamped the back page of Kafka's *The Trial* and handed it to me I remember how seriously I carried it home. It was as if I held my adulthood in the palms of my hands. Franz Kafka. His very name spoke to me of things I could already understand: of otherness, of Europe, of the feather-bedding we slept under (no woollen blankets like other school friends until Mama won ten pounds in Tatts one year), of schnitzel and of poppy-seed cake.

What I remember from that first reading is a story of a legal system that is bewildering to Kafka's protagonist, Josef K. He is sitting on his bed one morning, waiting for his breakfast to be delivered, when he is disturbed by a stranger in a suit, who is there to arrest him for a crime of which he is ignorant.

I understood Josef K. I found my childhood bewildering, and felt I had to seek out the meaning of the world independently from the explanations that were not forthcoming from my parents. When Josef K. says he is innocent of any crimes, his arrester says, 'That's what the guilty always say.' I felt, as many children do, that the unhappiness of my parents was due to something I might have done. Did I have a legion of unnamed crimes of which I thought I was innocent, but may, indeed, have been guilty?

Reading *The Trial* again, I am struck by how clearly and simply the story is told (in translation, of course) and by how much it has in common with Lewis Carroll's *Alice's Adventures in Wonderland*, a dream where events are more or less lifelike, but don't add up to anything sensible. But while Alice is in a world that is frustrating and bewildering, 'sentence first, verdict afterwards', Josef K. is seriously at risk.

Kafka describes each step that Josef K. takes and why: how he is childlike in his analysis of the people around him and of the insane events that unfold, his assumptions about his rights and how the system would work for him. I had no experience of formal bureaucracies, but I must have intuited, from my experience of school or my parents' experiences of factory life or of going to the bank for a loan, that he was heading for trouble.

I wonder now if I equated the grownupness of being

allowed to read the book with the grown-up world it described. Whatever the effect, Kafka gave me an early taste
for both absurdity and European writing that has never
left me.

Like many of my generation, my political reading
started with Aldous Huxley and George Orwell. *Animal
Farm* was a school text. And then I read *Nineteen Eighty-
Four.* I'm not sure how good the teaching was, or how well
I was paying attention, but I missed some of the lessons
embedded in these books. I understood the rewriting of
history by the state, its close observation of its citizens, and
its manipulation of language, but I didn't understand that
Orwell's state was not capitalist but socialist.

*Brave New World* was not a school text. Set in London
in 2540 AD, Aldous Huxley's novel describes a world
that is one big happy state. I read the opening pages and
the laboratory descriptions of the manufacture of children—the exact recipes for making everyone from clever
Alphas to hopelessly stupid Epsilons, the inoculation of
tropical workers with sleeping sickness and typhoid—and
I thought Huxley had come up with quite a good
system, especially as I regarded myself as an Alpha (I was
good at school and loved to learn). I could see the frustration of people like Mama, who was clever but completely
unschooled and therefore stuck with doing menial jobs,
and decided that special breeding programs might be

sensible. I'm not sure what I made of the soma and sex, but the class system stayed with me longer than anything else in the book. I thought of it as a system based on a meritocracy rather than on money and connections, overlooking the inequalities that were imposed well before birth.

I kept reading Orwell: *Down and out in Paris and London* and *The Road to Wigan Pier*, published in 1933 and 1937 respectively, and grew outraged at the mistreatment of the poor and the working classes. I think it was around this time, in my early teens, that I first heard of Karl Marx and Friedrich Engels.

When I was fourteen years old I bought *The Communist Manifesto* and read it in my room, excited by the frisson that came from its seemingly dangerous ideas. How could you not like a book that began 'A spectre is haunting Europe...' and ended with, more or less, 'Let the ruling classes tremble at a communist revolution. The proletarians have nothing to lose but their chains. They have a world to win. Proletarians of all countries, unite!'

Was I a proletarian? I thought so. My parents worked in factories and had no money. I had forgotten by then that I thought I was one of Huxley's Alphas as well.

In the meantime, Mama's couch reading had taken a decidedly political turn too. In August that year, Soviet tanks trundled into Prague. She handed me her copy of Yevgeny Yevtushenko's *Selected Poems* in which I read his most famous poem, 'Babi Yar', and she followed this with Alexsandr Solzhenitsyn's *One Day in the Life of Ivan Denisovich*, his novel of life in Soviet prison and labour camps. After that she gave me *Cancer Ward* and *The Gulag Archipelago*.

Now I think it is strange that Mama and I never discussed the content of these books. Perhaps it was because they were too close to the novels about Nazi concentration camps that I knew existed elsewhere but not in our house.

It was as if Mama was in a silent order where ideas and knowledge were passed between us with nothing but the text to speak. She semaphored. I interpreted. I have no idea if we were using the same code.

How I would have loved to speak with her about passages like this one from *Gulag*:

> If only it were all so simple! If only there were evil people somewhere insidiously committing evil deeds, and it were necessary only to separate them from the rest of us and destroy them. But the line dividing good and evil cuts through the heart of every human being. And who is willing to destroy a piece of his own heart?

Like Grace Paley, my mother marched in the moratorium against the Vietnam War in Melbourne in 1970. To my surprise I met her in Collins Street after I had absconded from maths with my school friends to march. Far from being cross with me, she seemed pleased that we had dis-covered what a radical housewife she was. This was long before I had read Grace Paley. As far as I knew, Mama voted Labor. But I also remember her telling me about an argument she had with one of the mothers at my sister's kindergarten, who became her close friend.

The woman had taken up the offer of a free university place that came in with the Whitlam government in 1972. She had enrolled in a politics degree and was discussing the Vietnam War with my mother and what it was the Vietnamese people themselves might want. My mother's friend said that they wanted Communist rule, but Mama said that people just wanted full bellies and would vote for whoever provided them with this. What did anyone know, I heard her say, who hadn't experienced war firsthand? Nothing.

That, of course, included me.

My friends and I were watching *M\*A\*S\*H* on televi-sion. We were reading Joseph Heller's *Catch-22,* set in World War Two, and laughing at the absurdities it describes. When Heller's hero, Yossarian, is asked to continue flying dangerous bombing missions, the only way he can get out of doing so is to plead insanity. But if you were insane, you wouldn't want to stop flying, so you must be sane to want to stop, in which case you have to keep flying. That's catch-22.

I also read *The Good Soldier Švejk,* written in 1923

by Jaroslav Hašek. Heroism, loyalty and justice are given a marvellously absurdist treatment in this novel set in Prague at the beginning of World War One. The main character Josef Švejk, previously a dealer in stolen dogs, joins the Czech army and becomes a batman to several officers. With a mixture of enthusiasm, idiocy and luck, he survives a war in which fifteen million people die. Somehow, with his misunderstandings and misplaced loyalties (or does he understand things all too well?) he manages to turn his setbacks into victories. He spends much of the time in the novel imprisoned—at one point, in a lunatic asylum. Here is what he makes of this experience:

> I'm blowed if I can make out why lunatics kick up such
> a fuss about being kept there. They can crawl about
> stark naked on the floor, or caterwaul like jackals, or
> rave and bite. If you were to do anything like that in an
> open street, it'd make people stare, but in the asylum
> it's just taken as a matter of course. Why the amount of
> liberty there is something that even the socialists have
> never dreamed of…I liked being in that asylum, I can
> tell you, and while I was there I had the time of my life.

I long suspected that my father was a Švejkian figure— a simple tailor with a fondness for telling jokes who had somehow survived a war in which many millions had perished. His life lessons included not volunteering for anything, not voicing political opinions to anyone and staying at the back of the room. The story he told me about the woodcutter and the bird with the golden heart rang true to all his subsequent advice.

The first story that I ever had published was in a collection about Australian Rules football called *The Greatest Game*. My story 'Thighs and Whispers' was about how I had never been to a football match, but had determined as a child that following a footy team was something that all children should do. The story began with a recollection of my father's extreme attitudes and how they applied to football teams. Living in St Kilda I intuited that it was the Right Thing to barrack for the St Kilda football team, even though I had no idea what that was. When I asked for a Saints scarf in red, white and black, like the other kids had, my father was very reluctant to buy one. As I type this, I realise that these are the colours of the Nazi flag too. But I think he was unhappy to make those sorts of statements, where, if the winds changed, he'd be in a difficult position. When I quizzed my parents about who they barracked for in Poland, my mother said they barracked for the winners—first for the liberation forces of the Red Army and then the occupation forces of the American Army.

I have been a member of several trade unions and had a brief stint in the ALP when I was asked to help write a women's health policy in the early 1980s (requiring me to become a member), but I am not naturally a joiner. It was not that I was afraid of being on the wrong team in the event of a conflict, but that I could always see many sides of an issue, and it was hard to convince myself that one lot had all the answers. Apart from that, my reading was underpinning my sense that, even with the best ideas, politics was full of manipulators and ne'er-do-wells who enjoyed playing backroom games to their own advantage. That even the best institutions were supported by vast idiotic bureaucracies, and that taking them on would lead to endless frustration.

In this vein I went on to read Austrian writer Thomas Bernhard's *Gathering Evidence: A Memoir*, Elias Canetti's *Auto-da-Fé* and the short stories of Swiss writer Robert Walser. These days there are many Russians who write absurdist anti-authoritarian satire, now that they can. Dmitry Bykov is one, and in his novel *Living Souls* he writes: 'No one could deny that the main purpose of every Russian government, whatever its character and duration, was to crush its citizens.' Bykov described to me the current Russian polity as a 'cold civil war' which is not so much about the murder of its citizens as destroying their brains.

Thirty years after I read *Catch-22* I found myself standing in Joseph Heller's Upper West Side Manhattan apartment in New York, overlooking Central Park. He was serving me tea and biscuits. While I interviewed him his fluffy little white dog ran in and out of the room.

In his memoir *Now and Then* he said that the short stories he was writing after his World War Two experience were plotted extravagantly and often 'resolved miraculously by some kind of ironic divine intervention on the side of the virtuous and oppressed'. So I asked him how this outlook evolved into a book where the exploiters triumph, and the good and deserving get nothing?

'What happened', he told me, 'is that my attitudes evolved in a Darwinian sense, and realism is realism, and what happens does happens, and what does happen in life is that the virtuous usually do not triumph, and those who are triumphant usually lack virtue, too often they lack conscience. It's the difference between being very young and having a belief in the miraculous, and being a little mature and educated and knowing there is no such thing as the miraculous.'

Heller did something very few writers do: he gave the English language a new word—catch-22. But there is one writer who is the epitome of a certain kind of political writing, no matter which language you are reading. His work seems to rise from the depths of empathy and wisdom.

Joseph Roth was born in 1894 in the Ukrainian city of Brody, then part of the Austrian Empire, in a poor region in which Jews, Poles and Ukrainians lived. He went to the University of Vienna in 1914 where he studied German Literature and began to write poems. After World War

One, in which he served with the Austro-Hungarian Army on the eastern front, he began to write for newspapers, in both Vienna and later in Berlin. When he was appointed Paris correspondent of the *Frankfurter Zeitung* he was one of the best-paid journalists in Germany.

Roth's greatest novel, which I read after I first encountered his journalism, is agreed to be *Radetzky March*, which follows three generations of the Trotta family: a soldier elevated to a position of nobility because of a brave act during a battle; an administrator; an army officer. The story of the family follows the fall of the Austro-Hungarian Empire—and the disillusionment of its supporters.

Poet, critic and translator Michael Hofmann has translated many of Roth's books into English, *Radetzky March* included, as well as a collection of his journalism, columns and studies called *What I Saw: Reports from Berlin, 1920–1933*. They are marvellous pieces, full of wit and depth, written with the novelist's eye for character and story, and a journalist's duty of witness.

Hofmann explained to me that Roth was always rather syncopated. 'He is a Jew in Austria, an Austrian in Germany, and a German in France. He is "red Roth" and a Habsburg loyalist; he is an Eastern Jew and an Austrian; he is gallant and passionate—both a kisser of hands and a kisser of feet; he is generous and unforgiving; he demands hope, and sees despair as a badge of reason.'

The collection includes the form that Roth made his own—the *feuilleton*, a short literary article said to be best at just a page, and written at a café table. Many of the pieces are from the earlier collection *Ein Lesebuch für Spaziergänger* (A Walker's Guidebook) and take us around 1920s Berlin:

> What I see…What I see is the day in all its absurdity and triviality. A horse, harnessed to a cab, not knowing that horses originally came into the world without cabs…I see a girl, framed in an open window, who is part of the wall and yearns to be freed from its embrace, which is all she knows of the world.

He walks the city thinking about traffic and railway crossings, visiting building sites or an auction of the exhibition of once-topical waxworks, writes profoundly about a sign in a railway carriage for 'Passengers with Heavy Loads', rides an escalator and visits homes for sick and destitute refugees. 'All state officials', he writes, 'should be required to spend a month serving in a homeless shelter to learn love.'

Can you imagine reading a line like that in a newspaper today?

And, although he was intensely interested in politics, he preferred to approach it from the sidelines, and through a kind of poetic expression. Defending his style to his editor at the *Frankfurter Zeitung* when he thought he was being sidelined he said, 'I'm not a garnish, not a dessert, I'm the main course.'

His prescience is heartbreaking. In the last piece in this collection, 'The Auto-da-fé of the Mind', written in 1933, he begins:

> Very few observers anywhere in the world seem to have
> understood what the Third Reich's burning of books,
> the expulsion of Jewish Writers, and all its other crazy
> assaults on the intellect actually mean…It must be
> understood. Let me say it loud and clear: the European
> mind is capitulating. It is capitulating out of weakness,
> out of sloth, out of apathy, out of lack of imagination (it
> will be the task of some future generation to establish
> the reasons for this disgraceful capitulation). Now, as
> the smoke of our burned books rises into the sky, we
> German writers of Jewish descent must acknowledge
> above all that we have been defeated. Let us, who
> were fighting on the frontline, under the banner of the
> European mind, let us fulfil the noblest duty of the
> defeated warrior; let us concede our defeat.

Roth left Berlin in 1933 and settled in Paris, finding it hard to survive. He was a refugee, his wife was in a mental hospital in Germany, and he was drinking and spending what little he had, arguing with publishers and begging friends for cash. 'And believe me, never did an alcoholic "enjoy" his alcohol less than I did. Does an epileptic enjoy his fits?

Does a madman enjoy his episodes?' he wrote to his friend Stefan Zweig.

In 1936 he was already describing himself as 'half madman, half corpse' and he failed to take up opportunities to escape to the United States. In 1939 he had come to the end. He died in a Paris hospital with pneumonia after days of delirium tremens. He was forty-four. He was saved the fate of many others, including his wife, who was killed the next year as part of Hitler's eugenics program.

I am moved by the tragedy of his life, by the beauty of his observations of the world around him, by his inability to save himself, by the silence he encountered in response to his political writings, even though he had a platform and was saying important things.

And I see now that if I gathered all my favourite absurdist and prescient European authors in one room I would have a group of variously mad, alcoholic, outrageous, obsessive men. Some of them would be friends with each other, many would have read each other's work. Loners and misfits often, I probably would not be interested in sharing their tables at the cafés and bars, or even having repeated conversations with them.

But I don't want to marry them. I only love what they wrote.

## CHAPTER 6

# Does Comrade Ivanov write English?

My mother was a polyglot who spoke to me in broken English. I had a smattering of Yiddish, the kinds of words you might learn for parts of the body when your mother dries you after a bath, but I couldn't construct a sentence. I knew some Polish swear words for archaic insults such as 'white cholera on you!' and 'dog's blood', and a Russian phrase for 'go fuck your mother'. When I asked her why she hadn't taught me other languages, Mama said that she wanted me to learn good English. And she wanted to learn it too. But I can't imagine communicating with my children in a language that I hadn't yet mastered. I think, now, that keeping from us the languages in which she could express everything she knew was part of her need for secrecy. Perhaps she feared us knowing all she had to tell.

71

## By the Book

On my bookshelves are the text books for the languages that I have formally tried to learn—Hebrew, Yiddish, German, French, Spanish and Russian.

The Russian books are the oldest. After reading *The Communist Manifesto*, and identifying myself as a proletarian, so keen was I to unite with the other proletarians that I decided to learn Russian. I could read the great political tracts and I could possibly work as a spy for the revolution too. They didn't teach Russian at Balwyn High, but they did offer it as a Saturday morning class at University High. I was fourteen and so I was allowed to go by myself. *Learning Russian, Books 1–4* by Nina Potapova are slim grey hardbacks. Inside, readers are invited to send any remarks or suggestions about the books to Progress Publishers, 21 Zubovsky Boulevard, Moscow, USSR.

I must have been pretty impressed to have a line of direct contact with the Soviet revolutionaries at Progress Publishers, and began to spend my Saturday mornings taking two trams from North Balwyn to the university, and then walking across the campus to the high school, for the lessons, before taking the same route home. The teacher was immaculate, with straight bleached blonde hair teased into some kind of helmet shape, white boots and stockings and a mini dress. It was the beginning of 1968 and she was serious, just as I thought she should be, since the revolution was not something you took lightly.

So now I could add a new alphabet to the two I already knew—English and Hebrew—and experience the endless fascination of learning a new language. I discovered in the first lesson that this one dropped the articles—you just said 'house', not 'the house' or 'a house', and you didn't have to use the English verb *to be* in the present tense—he here, bridge there.

But I was impatient. And you can't be impatient while learning a language or a new musical instrument. I was stuck with sentences like, 'Does Comrade Ivanov write English?' Or 'The river is on the left, the forest is on the right.' Or 'The air is fresh today!' How could I be a revolutionary if I was limited to such banalities?

I daydreamed that my teacher would recognise my radical potential and make some approach to draft me into a secret plan, but she did nothing of the sort. She favoured those who did their homework although she praised my accent. This came from listening all my life to people who were translating their own languages—including Russian—into broken English, and gave me scope for mimicry. It occurs to me now that neither of my parents, who both understood Russian (at least, as it related to their own Slavic language of Polish), offered to help me.

By the middle of the year I had dropped out of the Russian classes for the same reason that I had dropped my violin lessons. After a year of violin I couldn't play like

Isaac Stern and in the Russian class we were still limited to 'I remember all the words of the song about the mother-land' and 'the collective farm is being built by the workers'. I told my parents I had too much school homework to fit Russian in as well.

But the truth was that my revolutionary aspirations were not being nurtured by my teacher. Although I loved the freedom of spending most of Saturday crisscrossing the city on my own on the trams, my romantic dreams were being crushed, and this was unsustainable. I kept the books, of course, hoping that I would have the time to learn Russian again in the future.

My Russian lessons were preceded by French at high school and Hebrew before that at Sunday School. I loved learning new ways people had invented for communicating with each other. My language books are joined on the shelf by a slim volume, more a word list than a dictionary, that I was given on the eve of a trip to Papua New Guinea to write some newspaper columns. I was travelling with an aid agency worker. She and I were flying to a remote part of the country to investigate the effects of Japanese forest harvesters on the local landholdings.

There is nothing like curling up with a word list like this one in Tok Pisin. The language was developed in the early 1800s, an English-based creole which is now one of the three national languages of Papua New Guinea. I had colleagues at the ABC who broadcast in Tok Pisin to the region and I enjoyed hearing them talk to each other in the corridors. You had to speak the words aloud to detect their origin and many were clever and comical.

*Bras bilong teet*—toothbrush (brush belong teeth)

*Garas bilong het*—hair (grass belong head)

*Sop bilong garas*—shampoo (soap belong grass)

I was idly learning the language, as we were only going for a few days and would have a translator. He was a 23-year-old Tolai warrior and he met us on a remote landing strip. Our fifteen-seater plane took off again almost immediately and we were left, two women and one warrior, sitting on benches under a rough shade shelter.

We were waiting for a truck that was to take us to our accommodation for the next few days. It was very, very hot and our lift was very, very late.

Some hours and two litres of water later I needed to find a toilet. My word book was in the bottom of my pack and, anyway, I thought, this guy is the translator so why would I need to say what turned out to be *smolhaus i stap we?* As far as I could see there was no small house stopping anywhere and only long grass on either side of the runway.

So I turned to him and told him I needed to go for a walk into the long grass. He looked surprised. I showed him the empty water bottle and said it again. I stepped off the platform and said it once more. I had read enough anthropology books to know that there might be some kind of sacred place that I really shouldn't use as a toilet, so I asked him if he could show me where to go.

I was puzzled when he walked with me to the appointed spot. Did he want to protect me from snakes? When he wouldn't leave my side, I assumed he really was there to protect me. I had been bushwalking in mixed company before, and was wearing a long dress anyway, so, forced to obey my urgent bladder, I squatted down next to him. He surprised me by relieving himself in a strong stream. I put this down to cultural practices.

When I began to walk back to the platform, he seemed truly puzzled and asked me if I was ready to have enjoyments. Enjoyments? He asked if I was married.

I was not.

'So,' he asked, 'we can have enjoyments?'

'No, we can't have enjoyments,' I said. I was a journalist at work, there would be no enjoyments at all.

He told me that if I ever wished to have enjoyments I need only ask him.

I was confused until my friend told me that illicit sexual activity in the local villages happened away from the large common houses. Suggesting a walk into the 'long grass' was tantamount to asking a bloke back to your hotel for a 'drink' at midnight.

I am still puzzled by this, as my dictionary tells me

that 'having sex with a woman' is *hevim seks* or *wantaim meri*, but it is easy to find cross-cultural interactions confusing, especially if, like me, you like to put your language lessons into practice before you really know how to say much.

I have even managed to generate confusion in Canada, in the English-speaking city of Toronto, at a writers festival where you might expect to find experts in communication. I had arrived in Toronto fresh from New York, and was rubbing shoulders with the organisers and guests. There were some familiar faces there, and some new ones. I had missed my daily bout in the gym, so I was pleased when a kind-faced Canadian novelist leaned over and said, 'Have you been outside yet today, because I was thinking of going for walk.'

I sprang to my feet, agreed that it was a good idea, and told him to wait a minute while I got my coat.

We left the hotel and took the path that led around Lake Ontario, and conversed in a friendly fashion about buildings and water birds and Canada in general. After fifteen minutes I noticed with a broadcaster's ear that his language had subtly changed. He was now using the word 'we' in every third sentence, such as, 'We have a little house in the northern forests,' or 'When we decided to sell that car...'

We were sitting together on a park bench overlooking some Canada Geese as they swam on the lake when he asked me if I knew that his wife was arriving that night.

'No,' I said, somewhat puzzled. 'How would I know that?' I had just met him and had never met his wife.

My brain then engaged, and I realised that this man was trying to tell me something other than his wife's travel plans. He seemed to be asking me what my intentions were towards him, and if they were honourable. Given his nervousness, I asked him why he had invited me to come for a walk at all.

'I didn't,' he said.

Taken aback, I begged to differ. I explained that an Australian interpretation of what he'd said was: 'Have you been outside yet? (If you haven't, you might like to come now.) Because I was thinking of going for a walk. (Why don't you come too?)'

He said that in Canada, the phrase he used had meant: 'Have you been outside yet? (What's the weather like? Because there could be a blizzard and I could die.) Because I was thinking of going for a walk. (By myself.)'

Feeling rather defensive now—and noting to myself that it was sunny—I explained that in Australia if a bloke was telling a woman he wanted to go for a walk by himself he could expect one of two responses: One. Why don't you tell someone who cares, or Two. You poor bastard, hang on, I'll come and keep you company so you don't go and blow your brains out.

This wasn't the only introduction I had to Canadian mores. Another guest of the festival, Argentinian-born Alberto Manguel, told me a true story about a hold-up, where a man went into a shop, with only a Canada Goose under his arm, and said that he wanted money. If the woman behind the counter didn't cooperate, 'The goose gets it.' The shopkeeper gave him everything in the till, and even went down the street with him to her automatic teller machine to withdraw all of her savings. She handed him the cash, he handed over the goose, and ran off.

Manguel delighted in the story, and described how staggered his Argentinian friends were on hearing it. And it confirmed his decision to live in Canada and become a Canadian. If you had to choose between a country that 'disappeared' its people and one that preferred not to 'disappear' its geese, you'd become Canadian too.

# CHAPTER 7

## *Becoming a woman*

---

When I was a girl, my parents' friends admired me for my blonde hair and blue eyes, my 'good looks'. In their circle this meant that I would not automatically be assumed to be Jewish were the Nuremberg Laws of 1935 somehow to be enacted in faraway 1960s Australia. If my mother spoke of me getting one hundred per cent for maths, my father would remind her that this would not get me a husband. In fact, he said, if I grew much taller than I was at fifteen, my education would be held against me. He thought that most good Jewish boys were short like him, and wanted women shorter still. They didn't want to be towered over by a girl who could do algebra.

The agreed wisdom among the Friday night card-players who convened at our house every fourth week (playing Red Aces or Gin Rummy at four card tables with matches as the stakes) was that my mother read too many books, and that I was in danger of going the same way.

The piles of books consumed by the silent woman on the couch told another story. Betty Friedan's *The Feminine Mystique* was published in 1963, and by 1969, when I was fifteen, my mother passed it to me. It had become a bestseller and Friedan was by then the first president of America's National Organization for Women. She described the lives of women who had been college graduates but who were now trapped into suburban lives making homes and having babies. She called this 'the problem that has no name'. Friedan argued that the feminine mystique was a set of values that meant a woman's life could be fulfilled by looking after her husband, her children, her home and her looks. Women were expected to be dominated by their husbands, sexually passive, and to find emotional fulfilment in love for their children. Psychologists, advertisers and politicians were all in on this. 'Each suburban wife struggled with it alone,' Friedan wrote. 'As she made the beds, shopped for groceries…she was afraid to ask even of herself the silent question—"Is this all?"'

I was unsettled by this book. My mama had told my sister and me that she had never in her life been as happy and fulfilled as when we were born. Now she was saying, silently though it may have been, that there was more to life than looking after us. Maybe being our mother was marginally better than trying to survive in Warsaw during the Holocaust, but were we really holding her back from pursuing a life outside the confines of our kitchen and laundry? Betty Friedan's women had been educated in universities but Mama had not got past Grade 6. Was working in a factory or as an outworker at home better than making our lunches and ironing our school uniforms? What was she dreaming of as she read on our couch?

The sixties in Australia were probably like the fifties in Friedan's United States. Mama once arranged a mortgage to build a small factory on a pocket handkerchief of land she had bought in an inner-city slum suburb (she used money from her German repatriation pension, which she received as a survivor of the Holocaust), but when Dad heard about it he started to worry that she would lose everything, and went to the bank and cancelled the loan. He could do this because he was her husband and she needed his signature. I still remember the bitter fight that ensued.

I could see she was frustrated, and remember her tears. She was much more adventurous and better read than my father; it must have seemed like she was being held captive by a lesser being.

But I realised that my mother had given me *The Feminine Mystique* not so much to paint a picture of her own life as to allow me to plot the trajectory of mine. This was purely theoretical plotting at this stage—she was still buying my clothes and restricting my social life and would do so until, in the summer of the year I turned sixteen, I found a holiday job selling ladies swimwear in Myer's department store. After that she gave me a translation of French philosopher and novelist Simone de Beauvoir's *The Second Sex*, a more complex book. Its most memorable phrase was, 'One is not born, but rather becomes, a woman.'

De Beauvoir meant that we learned to be women, learned what was expected of us, how to walk and talk and be. This was a mystifying idea so soon after the changes that 'becoming a woman' (as my mother put it) had made to my body and to my concept of myself—I could have children now. If I wasn't a woman, what was I? And had I become a woman through simple biology or had society made me one?

Philosophy aside, I enjoyed reading de Beauvoir because she lived in Paris, the city where my parents had spent four years after the end of World War Two. The rare times that we could get Mama to talk about the past were when she baked. Between the dough being made and the yeast rising, I had a whiff of Paris after the war, when de Beauvoir and Sartre might lunch at Les Deux Magots in Saint-Germain-des-Prés. My mama, on the other hand, had a job as an outworker in a fourth-floor one-room apartment in another part of the city, but I fitted her story into my impressions as best I could.

Of course there was the other scandalous part of the life of Simone de Beauvoir—she was not married to Jean-Paul Sartre and they both took lovers. She had no children. But for many of my generation they were the couple who served as a model for the kind of life that might be possible—he the founder of existentialism and she one of the pioneers of feminism. They lived as equals and they travelled together and helped each other develop ideas for their books. They valued freedom and honesty and dismissed jealousies.

Anyway, that was the theory—one that has taken a beating in the years since my friend, the late Hazel Rowley, published her book *Tête-à-Tête: Simone de Beauvoir & Jean-Paul Sartre* in 2005. Rowley describes the lies and jealousies and unhappiness that the couple never publicly admitted. She reveals that Sartre used to promise to marry the 'drowning women' he took as mistresses—'these rather neurotic little women, often actresses, very beautiful always, whom he took under his wing and made financially dependent on him and he wrote plays for them, which they weren't always up to'. Meantime Simone de Beauvoir, the one who could swim, kept insisting that marriage was not what they wanted, and that she was the most important woman in his life.

But all this was beyond me when I was a teenager. I did notice that, much to my irritation, my father was right about boys and me and mathematics, but I didn't care very much as I loved school and I loved having my head in books too. And who cared about the boys in my class? I had no way of meeting those more interesting-looking older boys anyway, as Mama was still very strict.

But that didn't stop her from casually leaving Mary McCarthy's novel *The Group* on the bookshelf. Where of course I found it. The book, first published in the United States a few months after *The Feminine Mystique*, while not officially banned, had been the subject of a threat to prosecute booksellers and a subsequent campaign in Victoria by the 'Freedom to Read' group. It explores the lives of eight women who graduate from Vassar College in 1933. They embark on sex, love, marriage and motherhood and one of them takes a lesbian lover. I remember being intrigued by the pen-portraits of the women on the back cover.

> Lakey—Mona Lisa of the smoking room—for women only!

> Libby—a big red scar in her face called a mouth.

> Dottie—Thin women are more sensual. The nerve ends are closer to the surface.

Really? Was that true about thin women? Whatever kind

of woman I was going to be, it wasn't thin. Was I destined not to be sensual? What was sensual anyway? It was hard to read the book in snatches when Mama was in the kitchen or out shopping.

The only really vivid part I remember was when Dottie, the thin one, goes to get a pessary from the doctor after her rather unsatisfactory defloration with Dick, who didn't kiss her at all. Armed with her pessary she waits in Washington Square Park for him to meet her for their next assignation, but he doesn't turn up so she leaves the contraceptive device under the bench and walks away. As if she has had a narrow escape from Dick as well as the pessary.

I wonder if reading this led to my own shyness about contraception when I went to university in 1972. The pill had been available for years by then, and even my best friend's mother was on it. I was confused by this. All of the talk in the press was about the pill and how racy single girls were being prescribed it, but as my parents had separate rooms I had no occasion to ask my Mama about contraception. And we both knew I didn't need contraception to read, and that was all I was allowed to do, so what was there to talk about?

I fear that I thought that the Vassar class of '33 rules applied to my first year of university. I would have saved myself a lot of heartache if I had marched up to the Student Health Clinic and got myself sorted as soon as I enrolled. I blame Mary McCarthy and a fundamental misreading of her novel.

For despite my wide reading, I was completely sheltered. I caught the bus to university each day, attended my classes, borrowed books from the library and made my way home. This was my pattern until I started 'going out' in first year with a medical student who was a few years older and who knew everything there was to know about life on campus. And life in general. Or so I thought.

How silly I was. In 1973, in my second year of university, when I was eighteen, I told my mother I had a university excursion and got up early, met my boyfriend on our street corner, and we hitchhiked to a private hospital in the suburbs, where I had an abortion. The doctor was kind, and wore black-and-white platform shoes. My boyfriend left me there and went off to buy me flowers. Later we took a taxi back to university where we sat in the cafeteria for the afternoon. He walked me to the bus stop and I went home. My mother was none the wiser.

My perspective shifted. I thought of myself as damaged goods. Whatever my education had done to limit my attractiveness to nice Jewish boys, I had now written myself off completely. I was no longer a virgin and had had an abortion too. The campus was in the throes of the women's movement, and I read *Sisterhood Is Powerful*, a collection of writings edited in 1970 by the American poet and activist Robin Morgan. It contained essays by Kate Millett and Mary Daly, and poems and articles about lesbians and prostitutes, and the SCUM manifesto railing against men. I saw leaflets in the cafeteria asking for volunteers for a group called the Abortion Law Reform Association (ALRA), and joined up.

Every couple of weeks I went to a first-floor address on Fitzroy Street in St Kilda, which in the daytime was an ordinary office and at night became the centre for telephone-counselling services. We waited for calls from women who were pregnant. We'd ask them which suburb they lived in and then give them the phone number and address of the nearest sympathetic GP, who would declare that the woman's psychological or physical health was in danger if the pregnancy continued, qualifying her for an abortion. The idea was to spare women the humiliation of being refused the help of one doctor after another. I'm not sure if what we were doing was legal or not, but it sure felt undercover. St Kilda was full of prostitutes and drug dealers, not that I saw many of them. There was a leaflet by the phone telling us what to do if the police raided the office, but I never had to use it.

I can't remember what I told my mama but I'm sure she thought I was still studying in the library. I'm now imagining what she might have done had I rung her from the police watchhouse after I had been arrested, the daughter who just a year or two before was dutifully putting on the clothes she had bought for me. But I think by then she was probably trying to work out how to tell us she was fatally ill.

During the next term my friend from ALRA, who was also my laboratory partner in second-year biochemistry, suggested I come to a consciousness-raising group at her share house. I attended a few meetings. Most of the women were older than we were. Some were married, or about to be not married any more. They seemed to be a very unhappy group. They were just beginning to share their stories with each other, mostly of failed hopes and dreams. I did think of *The Feminine Mystique* and *The Group*. My reading had prepared me for these women, as had my observations of the life my mama led. But they had not been prepared for me.

They were moving into large women-only share houses, wearing overalls and beginning to shear off their hair. I lived with my parents, was fond of floor-length gingham or flower-print dresses and I wore my hair long to my waist. I told the women about my abortion, which they were sympathetic about, and of my kind boyfriend who bought me flowers, which they were not sympathetic about. I did not seem to understand that I was being oppressed. Each meeting left me more and more out in the cold. I felt their disapproval. I dropped out of the group.

Years later several of the women had succeeded in finding their true selves. They were lesbians by then and had made the difficult move to come out. I was in the wrong place at the wrong time: an incurable heterosexual, living in the past. I wasn't really paying attention to women such as Simone de Beauvoir any more. She had said, 'Why one man rather than another? It was odd. You find yourself involved with a fellow for life just because he was the one that you met when you were nineteen.'

That was precisely the direction I took. In 1973 I took a copy of *Down among the Women* by Fay Weldon with me when my medical-student boyfriend and I went north by train to a town on the Burdekin River in North Queensland where he had a summer posting in a hospital. When I wasn't studying for my supplementary exam in biochemistry, I read Weldon's comic novel. Beginning in 1950 (I was now clearly moving through history at a pace), it is about a group of women in London who have variously been left alone and pregnant, or married to much older men, or waiting for marriage or giving up work for marriage, or having an affair with a married man. But the women turn against and betray each other because they want to please the men in their lives.

The town we were living in was stuck in the early 1950s when it came to relations between the sexes, and in the 1920s when it came to relations between Aborigines and the townsfolk. It didn't take long for us to understand that there was a bar where the upper-class whites drank, and another one for white scum. The blacks were served at the back of the second pub, where white men of all classes met black women who'd go with them into the bushes. That is how it was explained to me.

My boyfriend and I were pretending to be married so that we could share a visiting doctor's house in the hospital grounds. The resident doctor saw that his southern student was competent, and withdrew to his own house to go on a bender lasting several weeks. The Aboriginal population heard that there was a new doctor in town who was open and kind and they began to line up in long queues to see him.

I was trying to study, but it was hard to concentrate. North Queensland was terribly hot and strange. And the wives of the dentist, accountant, lawyer and newsagent began to invite me to morning teas and generally give me the impression that I was a junior member of the upper white team.

The night of the hospital Christmas dinner-dance came. It was to be held in the top pub. My mother had finally stopped trying to dress me. She had made no suggestions about the clothing I might need in a tropical climate and I had nothing suitable to wear—certainly not the lime-green long-sleeved shirt and black jeans that were my only option. The ladies were all spruced up and the men were in pressed white shirts. The band played covers of fifties rock-and-roll hits and occasional Beatles songs.

After the speeches from the hospital administrator the music started and in the corner of my eye I saw an Aboriginal man in a light suit—could it have been violet?—making his way across the dance floor. I saw all the eyes in the room swing towards him. He was heading my way. He stopped at my seat and asked if I wanted to dance. His front two teeth had been knocked out. Now I think it the possible result of a ritual ceremony, but then it looked like he'd been brawling.

I could see the panic in my boyfriend's eyes. I was his woman, his pretend wife for the duration of the summer, and all the good burghers of the town were looking at us. But I was so impressed with the courage of the young man, with his audacity, that I jumped up from my seat and took his hand.

We danced and he told me he was up from Sydney, from Kings Cross, to see his family for Christmas. He was a little drunk, it was true, but he was a great dancer, and I remember thinking he must be gay. And slowly the dance floor emptied until we were the only ones there, and then the band stopped playing halfway through a song. He bowed low and I said thanks for the dance. He left the room as I took my place back at the table at the side of my beau, who was livid.

No one spoke to us and, soon after, we went back to our little house and had a huge argument. I explained that I was acting in support of the man fighting against the racism of the town and he explained that I was racist because I would never have danced with a strange man who was drunk and had no front teeth if he had been white. He said I had shamed him. Now everyone would think he could not control his woman.

And even with all the books I had read and the lessons I had tried to learn and the voices of the women in the consciousness-raising group and the words of Simone de Beauvoir and Mary McCarthy ringing in my ears, reader, I married him.

## CHAPTER 8

# Beauty is truth,
# truth beauty

I was nine years old. I was reading a children's compendium of famous women that I had taken out of the bus library—Cleopatra, Florence Nightingale, Joan of Arc—when I came upon a potted biography of Polish-born physicist and chemist Marie Curie. It was winter, I was wearing a cosy nightie done up to the neck as the thought dawned on me that this woman, with fair curly hair like mine and a blouse buttoned up to a high-necked collar, was, like my parents, Polish by birth, but that being Polish didn't mean that you inevitably worked, liked my parents, from dawn to dusk in clothing factories or at the treadle machine late at night in our kitchen. My fate was decided.

None of the immigrants in my parents' circle had professional jobs. One or two, it was rumoured, had gone to university for a few years before history sent them to concentration camps or to refuges of various kinds, and then to their lives in Melbourne at the end of the world. Tailors, furriers, milk-bar owners, greengrocers and truck-drivers, they all had ambitions for their Australian-born children. The boys would be doctors, lawyers, accountants or perhaps architects, and girls like me might be teachers before we got married, had children and helped our husbands in their careers. Not that it was spelled out to me like this, but a child sees what the world is like from the confines of the family, and we didn't exactly have wide horizons to survey. Except, of course, for those found in books.

Maria Skłodowska, as she was then, was born in 1867 into a Warsaw family. Her father, who was a high school teacher of physics and mathematics and a lover of poetry, and her mother, who was the headmistress at a school for girls, must have encouraged her interests. It was a completely different life from that led by women in my ancestral Polish family—they were orthodox Jewish mothers and wives, living in tiny shtetls, the mostly Jewish villages in the Polish countryside, running farms and shops and having many children while their husbands studied the Torah. The arc of their lives had probably not changed much since the seventeenth century.

During the day Maria Skłodowska worked as a governess and a teacher and, in the evenings, at the laboratory of the Warsaw Museum of Industry and Agriculture, learning chemical analysis and laboratory procedures. She became active in Polish nationalistic politics, and left for Paris in 1891 to study physics and mathematics at the Sorbonne. There she met the man who was to become her husband and collaborator, Pierre Curie. Together they worked in difficult conditions stirring great vats of pitchblende to isolate the new radioactive elements of radium and polonium.

In 1903, with Pierre and Henri Becquerel, Marie was awarded a Nobel Prize for physics for their work in radioactivity, and in 1911 she was given another, this one in chemistry. Even though I had not much understanding of the sociological differences between Marie Curie's family and mine, I remember thinking that I had so much in common with her that I might win a Nobel Prize too.

I set up an experimental laboratory in my mother's laundry. Someone gave me a small blue toy microscope for my tenth birthday. Where did I read that you could grow germs in some special gel? I assembled a variety of jars with pineapple jelly at the bottom, and I used the cat as the source of my test samples—I dipped her paws into the gel, took swabs from her ears and I even attempted to culture her milk, as she had given birth to a litter of kittens. I tried to work out the problem of milking a cat by lying alongside her kittens and watching how they pumped either side of her teats with their paws. I did the same and tried to taste her milk. Alarmed at the prospect of suckling a human child, she hid her kittens under the house for several weeks.

My mother was alarmed too when she saw what had grown in my jars over the weeks between me setting up the experiments and then forgetting about them. She ordered them out of her laundry. My other experiment involved getting the starch out of potatoes but she wasn't keen to use it in her washing. My father suggested it would be more useful if I made potato latkes instead.

I was intrigued by the world beyond what we could see with our naked eye. I took up science at high school and became good at mathematics and physics and chemistry. I loved imagining what the electrons and neutrons were doing in the atoms that made up everything around me. I loved the certainty that the 'universal laws of physics' implied, and thrilled to the idea that everything had an explanation, if only we could work out what it was. Elegant simplicities were the beautiful results of sheer brainpower and experimental design. Or so I thought.

But there were very few women scientists among those we studied.

One of my favourite stories about science and research was *The Double Helix: A Personal Account of the Discovery of the Structure of DNA* by James D. Watson, published in 1968. It told the heroic story of how Watson, together with Francis Crick and Maurice Wilkins, discovered the structure of the essential key to life. DNA was a beautiful, simple double helix, and it was made of four nucleotides—thymine, cytosine, adenine and guanine—which together coded everything that made a human being, or a spider, or a banana or a flower or anything alive you care to think of. I adored the idea of DNA and relished the inside story of how these scientists came to light upon this elegant shape. Watson's book was a bestseller, and I bought my copy at our newsagent.

The story begins in 1951 when Watson, a 23-year-old American, arrives with his newly minted doctorate at the famous Cavendish Laboratory in Cambridge. The laboratory is headed by Australian-born Nobel Prize–winning physicist and professor of experimental physics, Sir Lawrence Bragg, who even has a law named after him—Bragg's Law of X-Ray diffraction. It's a thrill for Watson to be there to study bacterial viruses and walk the same laboratory floors as the greats before him. It was a thrill for me to read about the places in which these great ideas were hatched.

Francis Crick is introduced, a 35-year-old English doctoral student of proteins, also at the Cavendish, and Maurice Wilkins, who is thirty-five too, and is looking at the structure of DNA using biochemical and biophysical methods at another laboratory at King's College, London.

With these chaps is Rosalind Franklin, a 31-year-old English physicist who, with Wilkins, is making photos of DNA using X-Ray diffraction. In this era, women and men didn't even share a lunch room. I was intrigued to find a woman in the story, but as the book unfolded I was a bit dismayed at how she was depicted. I didn't know any better than to believe Watson's view of Franklin.

> By choice she did not emphasise her feminine qualities. Though her features were strong, she was not unattractive and might have been stunning had she taken even a mild interest in clothes. This she did not. There was never lipstick to contrast with her straight black hair, while at the age of thirty-one her dresses showed all the imagination of English blue-stocking adolescents.

Rosalind Franklin, or 'Rosy' as Watson called her—she was not amused—was typecast as a cold, sexless, grumpy, challenging female scientist. Watson's view of her reminded me of that classic scene in old movies that were shown on daytime television when I was sick at home from school, in which a librarian or a bossy nurse wore glasses, but when the hero disarmed her with flirting and took her glasses away there stood a beauty in all her glory. Her demeanour changed immediately. He fell for her and she started swooning and forgot whatever fierce interests she had held. Presumably the world beyond the end of her nose became a blur, but he would do the seeing for both of them from then on.

Watson wrote about the bad blood between Franklin and Wilkins in their London laboratory, describing her as Wilkins' troublesome assistant. In truth she was getting on with her own part of the research. Wilkins passed on Franklin's work to Watson and Crick in Cambridge without her knowledge. This led to their confirmation of DNA as a double-helix structure and a Nobel Prize for the three men in 1962. By then Rosalind Franklin had died of ovarian cancer at the age of thirty-seven in 1958.

*Rosalind Franklin and DNA* was written by Anne Sayre in 1975 as a corrective to the portrait painted by Watson. At the time I was trying to juggle a new baby with an honours year in a microbiology laboratory, so I missed the book, but Sayre, who knew Franklin, could not reconcile the woman she knew with the caricature she had read, 'the female grotesque we have all been taught either to fear or to despise'.

She too noticed the way Watson muses on how Rosy might look if he removed her glasses. But, she informs us, Franklin not only always wore lipstick, she never wore glasses at all as she had brilliant eyesight and only used a magnifying glass for the finest of work.

Despite the danger that my interest in science would turn me into an unattractive old maid, the pull of the ideas was too strong for me. I read Desmond Morris's *The Naked*

*Ape*, Isaac Asimov's *I, Robot* and *Silent Spring* by Rachel Carson. I bought a book called *Check Your Own I.Q.* by Hans Eysenck, published in 1966, well before the controversies that would dog him over his views about race and intelligence, and tobacco-industry support of his research. I spent many an afternoon on my bed, testing, testing, testing. I announced to Mama that I had an IQ of 165, but I may have cheated.

I was immensely attracted to the order of things in physics and chemistry, like the periodic table of elements and the laws of physics. How marvellous to think that the world could be made of predictable actions and reactions, that this chemical mixed with that one always produced this reaction; that this particle aimed at speed at this surface would always be reflected and refracted in calculable ways. Of course this wasn't necessarily the case in every situation, but I was to learn that later. I was disturbed about the theory of light, refusing to accept that it sometimes behaves like a particle and other times as a wave. I was an all-or-nothing girl. I applied my mind to learning how the rules worked to predict the behaviour of the universe the same way I'd explored how the world worked through reading.

I failed my first-year university biology exam. I had been spending a lot of time in the gardens behind the Botany school with my boyfriend and a bottle of cheap port. When it came to the exam, the question was about the excretory system of the spider. All I could remember was that the spider had a bottom made of chitin—a plastic-like substance produced by mother nature to be so strong that the spider could excrete straight ammonia without it being transformed into urea, unlike us, who need the urea cycle to protect our own bottoms made of mere human flesh, or that's how I had understood it.

So, instead of writing a short biochemical analysis, I waxed lyrical on the beauty and profundity of this. Later I was hauled before the university Failures Committee.

'Have you,' my professor asked me, 'considered journalism as a career?'

Which I took as an insult because I was going to be Marie Curie. It was quite a long time before I came to see his point.

I spent a few years studying genetics and microbiology, and clearly my reading of *The Double Helix* had inspired me greatly. I was impressed with what we could find out about the world beyond our senses—what was too small or too far away to see. But I could never become Madame Curie with my baby in a bassinet under the bench, as my thesis supervisor told me one Sunday afternoon. I took my baby home and cried.

But I got over the grief because I realised that, with or without a baby, I didn't have the temperament to be really good at science. I was not graced with the kind of mind that revelled in working out the next step in a research project. I did not have the patience to stay with an idea, repeating and refining experiments. Many of the best researchers have an obsessive streak, a love of completeness, which drives them to do exactly that to push their knowledge further.

I was still impatient, and most of all I loved the poetry in these great stories of science. The miniature battles within our bloodstreams between invading antigens and our home armies of specialised defender cells were as exciting as any war story, full of strategy and risk. Imagining the tiniest dance of DNA strands as they were read by enzymes for translation was as mysterious and thrilling as the cosmic sweep in the movement of galaxies. And I loved the human drama at the centre of it all, of our ancestors looking up into the night sky and telling themselves stories of how the world came into being, reading the patterns of the stars and the visits of comets.

Poetry and science would not seem at first glance to have too much in common, not even the same language. Science stood accused of destroying whatever it was investigating in order to analyse it. As Wordsworth famously put it, 'We murder to dissect.' But the great poet Goethe was also a scientist. He is best remembered for his literary works like *The Sorrows of Young Werther* and *Faust*, but with his scientific imagination he made a significant contribution to biology.

He was an accomplished botanist and helped found the field of comparative anatomy, he invented the term *morphology*, and he even anticipated the theory of evolution. In 1784 he discovered the intermaxillary bone in the human jaw, thus supplying a link to primate anatomy that proved crucial to later evolutionary theories.

The English Romantic poets grappled with science in its fully modern sense. With the Industrial Revolution well underway, the Romantic generation experienced the chief distinguishing characteristic of modern science: its link to technology and its effort to transform the world in material terms.

We think of them as nature poets, and remember how appalled they were by how the beautiful landscape of England was made ugly by the scars of industrialisation. But Wordsworth also speculated that science might open up imaginative possibilities for poetry. And both Shelley and Byron were fascinated by what was happening in astronomy and cosmology. They took a special interest in the emerging fields of geology and palaeontology, and kept up with the latest theories about the prehistoric creatures that came to be known as dinosaurs.

One writer who brings the excitement of this time to life is the marvellous English biographer Richard Holmes. I was instantly a fan from his first book, *Footsteps: Adventures of a Romantic Biographer*, in which he retraces Robert

Louis Stevenson's 1878 journey through the Cévennes in southern France, goes to revolutionary Paris in pursuit of Wordsworth and Mary Wollstonecraft, and follows Shelley and his friends to Casa Magni, Shelley's house on the North Italian bay of Lerici. *Footsteps* was hailed as a milestone in biography for Holmes' insistence on locating long-forgotten stops on ancient journeys, and for the way he tells us what his subjects might have thought and felt in those places.

A more recent book of his is *The Age of Wonder: How the Romantic Generation Discovered the Beauty and Terror of Science*, referring to the period between 1770 and 1830, commonly called the Romantic Age. It was a time of grand explorations and discoveries: a new planet, a new way of travelling and seeing the world by air, and a new way of looking at the make-up of matter itself. It was indeed an age of wonder not only to those who worked in science but to its great writers.

Holmes starts with the botanist Joseph Banks who sailed with Captain James Cook on the *Endeavour* in the 1768 expedition to the South Pacific, and uses him as a trope of the romantic figure throughout his story. Holmes draws a portrait of Banks as a young man of twenty-five, who had an expensive education at Oxford and inherited a lot of money. His peers would have embarked on the Grand Tour of Europe with their servants. 'Any blockhead can do that,' Banks said. 'I'm going to go round the world.'

Judging from the portrait of Banks, which we saw at school, painted when he was much older, the man who collected plants had seemed to me a deeply boring character. I was never fascinated by plants, even as a science student. But reading Holmes made me want very badly to meet Banks, especially on that trip with Cook to Tahiti to observe the transit of Venus across the sun, which would help astronomers work out the distance between the Earth and the sun.

He is one of the first Europeans to land on the beach in Tahiti (twenty years before William Bligh and the *Bounty* mutineers and sixty-six years before Charles Darwin and the *Beagle*), and from this moment on he's open to everything. And he can do everything. Some days he does a bit of astronomy, a bit of exercise, a bit of botany, and then he thinks about the structure of the whole world.

They're in Tahiti for three months. The idea of the superior enlightenment of European civilisation begins to melt down for Banks as he discovers elements of this new civilisation that are immensely attractive. He has a wonderful expedition up country with one of the Tahitian queens who is smitten with him, and they share a canoe one night. But when Banks wakes up in the morning the locals have stolen almost everything—his brass-buttoned jacket, breeches and pistols have humiliatingly gone.

Banks is thrilled with the sexual opportunities in Tahiti and he considers the women there perfect in body and temperament for such delightful pastimes. Unlike his fellow travellers he tries to learn Tahitian, and Holmes suggests his lexicon reflects his passions: plants and animals, astronomical terms, the names for intimate parts of the body. He learns the words for stealing, understanding, eating and being angry or tired.

Banks became president of the Royal Society in 1778, an office he held for forty-two years, enough time to be painted with an Order of Bath across his chest, and looking most unlike the man who had danced naked with Tahitian girls on that long-ago beach in paradise. But Banks became a wonderful patron, sending young explorers in all the different areas of science around the world. One of these was the German astronomer William Herschel, who went on to discover Uranus.

Lord Byron had looked through Herschel's telescope. The young Percy Bysshe Shelley, who from the time he was a young student had microscopes and telescopes, read the Herschel papers. He noted the discovery of Uranus and the size of the universe, and was excited because, if there were many galaxies and solar systems, there must be many other planets. And other civilisations.

So Shelley asked himself about the role of God in all this. 'His works,' he said, 'have borne witness against him.'

Since I loved stories like those that Holmes tells I realised that it might suit me better to be a translator from the laboratories of scientists to the general public. To convey my excitement and to use language simply to interpret the jargon that many scientists were trained to use.

Scientists often complain that they are misquoted by journalists when they are interviewed. Journalists complain that they can't get a straight answer from scientists—that they are always qualifying themselves, making it difficult to work out what the story actually is. After my hopes to do scientific research were truncated by my circumstances and my personality, and my subsequent exposure to a few months working in medical microbiology (where people expected you to analyse rather disgusting bodily fluids and worse), I found a job teaching medical laboratory technicians at RMIT. From here I could put myself between scientists and journalists, as the campus has a close relationship with the community radio station 3RRR. In 1979 I started a weekly science program with a colleague. We called it *The Marie Curiosity Show*.

It gave me an excuse to read more books about science.

I read Stephen Jay Gould's books on natural history, physicist Paul Davies' many books on cosmology and the nature of the universe, *A Brief History of Time: From the*

*Big Bang to Black Holes* by Stephen Hawking, and James Gleick's *Chaos: Making a New Science*. Dava Sobel's book *Longitude: The True Story of a Lone Genius who Solved the Greatest Scientific Problem of His Time*, on the eighteenth-century invention of a clock that could tell the time at sea, was a landmark book in popular science.

Later, working for the ABC, I set myself challenges on radio. Could I explain complex ideas to lay audiences? None was as great as my interview with Roger Penrose, emeritus professor of mathematics at Oxford, who shared the Wolf Prize for physics with Stephen Hawking, for their joint contribution to our understanding of the universe.

The occasion was his appearance at the Edinburgh International Book Festival with his book *The Road to Reality: A Complete Guide to the Laws of the Universe*, a great tome that included many mathematical formulae and illustrations, penned by the author, of different possible universe evolutions, or 'quantum superpositions of alternative classical paths in configuration space'. Or the Newton/Carson spacetime. And they are the easy ones.

But for the interested general reader there were chapters and paragraphs of descriptive prose that gave a sense of what the shining mathematical formulae point to. *The Road to Reality* was described by *Wired* magazine as 'a mathematical *Finnegans Wake*'.

I tried to understand the book without understanding

the mathematics, and indeed Penrose had given permission for just such a reading in his introduction. He used terms such as *music, beauty, intuition, miracle* and *simplicity,* which you don't always associate with complex mathematics and physics. It seemed that there was a fundamental yearning in mathematics for the beauty of simplicity and the aesthetic attraction of coherence. I understood that. I was looking for it myself.

Penrose told me there was a very close relationship between beauty and truth. If there was a choice between two possibilities, one that would be a neat solution and another that might be messy, the likelihood is that the neater possibility is the true one, that beauty is the guide to what is true. It was, of course, the Romantic poet John Keats who said, in his 'Ode on a Grecian Urn':

'Beauty is truth, truth beauty'—that is all
Ye know on earth, and all ye need to know.

It's clear that human beings find certain things beautiful. Symmetry, for example—the faces that we find beautiful are the more symmetrical ones. And we are fond of order. It's the way we learn to navigate the world. Our brain labels things that are like each other and stores them together.

I was glad to find that my search for order and coherence was fundamental to my human mind, and not just a symptom of neurosis. Along the way I'd made another discovery too—how much I enjoyed making radio programs.

I had heard my own recorded voice as a child, on a reel-to-reel recorder owned by the father of a friend I'd made at Hebrew School. I thought they were a rich family, as they had a double-storey house, and the tape recorder confirmed this. We played with the machine, and I wondered how the tape captured the sounds. I'd forgotten how much fun I'd had making strange noises and hearing them back again.

Encouraged by my amateur beginnings at 3RRR where I learned to edit magnetic tape with a razor blade and a white chinagraph pencil, and to record interviews on temperamental cassette players, I finally left laboratories and students behind and embarked on a full-time career in radio journalism.

The studio control panels were filled with all kinds of mysterious buttons and switches and volume slides like those I imagined in extraterrestrial spaceships. I liked learning to operate the equipment but most of all I loved the intimacy of the conversations that you could have with strangers in the studio or at the end of telephone line or a satellite link. And these conversations could be heard across the country and across the planet.

I could ask the best minds in any field any questions that I liked. And if I had diligently read everything I could to understand the work they were doing they always gave me the best of answers. I began the kind of reading that immerses you in a subject, and I supplemented this with reading everything that had been written about the person I was going to interview. They became my quarry, and I tried to anticipate as much as I could about the exchange before we met. I was happily immersed in reading both the work and the mind that had made it.

## CHAPTER 9

# *Mortal men*

---

I had lived without a mother for nearly twenty years, and should have been able to look after myself, but just before I turned forty I slipped on a step and broke my ankle badly. The break had a name, a Pott's fracture, and it led to a series of medical problems that landed me in an intensive care unit. I was one of the only conscious patients, and I had little to do but lie down and breathe oxygen from a tank. I had trouble concentrating, but I asked my friend to bring me a book I'd bought years before and hadn't yet read.

Reading Oliver Sacks in a hospital seems only right. The book was *A Leg to Stand On*, his 1984 account of breaking his leg after an encounter with a Norwegian bull, and subsequently finding that his leg had suffered some neurological damage. This was especially distressing when he discovered his leg in his hospital bed with him and his damaged nerve told him it belonged to someone else. I was completely engrossed in the book; it was all about me.

When I left the hospital I noticed everyone in plaster or a wheelchair or with crutches or a walking stick. I loved watching the film *The Accidental Tourist*, the story of a man whose son is killed in an accident and whose marriage disintegrates. All I really remember of the film, though, was that he has a fall and is encased in plaster. I felt at one with William Hurt, the lead actor in the movie.

My fracture renewed my admiration for Sacks, the neurologist and writer whose work takes us into hospitals and consulting rooms, where his patients not only disclose a remarkable array of symptoms but reveal stories of their illnesses that give us an understanding of what it might be like to be them. And what it is like to be us.

I first met Oliver Sacks when he came to Melbourne on a book tour in the early 1990s. He was a bear of a man, with a great bushy beard and a wrestler's build. He was engaging but a little remote. When he arrived in my studio for a live-to-air interview he sat opposite me and took out of his bag what I thought was a large poultry thermometer and placed it in front of him.

Just before we went on air, I asked what the thermometer was for, and he explained that he is sensitive to heat.

He told me he might have a strange response—difficulty in speaking, for example—if the temperature went over 65 °F. I suggested he put it away until after the interview, since he might not be affected if he didn't know the exact temperature. He assured me the thermometer was not for him—he knew exactly when the temperature climbed to 65—it was for other people who might try to tell him the temperature was fine.

On another occasion I was interviewing him at a public event. He had asked for two huge fans to be placed in the wings of the stage. The fans were going full blast. The day was very warm and I was alarmed to see several trickles of sweat begin to make their way down Sacks's face. Could we reach the end of the interview before his distress became too great? When we got to audience question time, I breathed a sigh of relief. Sacks was on his own.

His best-known book is *The Man who Mistook his Wife for a Hat and Other Clinical Tales*. It came out in 1985 and was the first of his books I read. It is written in the 'case-study' approach made popular by Sacks's medico-literary antecedents Sigmund Freud and Russian neuropsychologist A. R. Luria. Sacks says that reading Luria's *The Mind of a Mnemonist: A Little Book about a Vast Memory* altered the focus and direction of his life. The book, translated into English in 1968, is an extended case study of a man with an extraordinary facility for remembering things, or perhaps a terrible affliction in not being able to forget anything.

Another of Luria's books, *The Man with a Shattered World: The History of a Brain Wound,* published in 1973, followed the case of a World War Two veteran, Sublieutenant Zasetsky, who sustained a bullet wound in 1943 that damaged the left side of his brain and caused memory, perception and language problems. Zasetsky was encouraged to write about his injury and its effects for twenty-five years, even though he could not read what he had written. These books, which attempt to tell the reader what it was like from the inside of the affliction, were described by Luria as 'romantic science'.

Sacks's writing brings us right into his medical rooms, and allows us to meet the patients as he did. We see through his eyes and make the connections he does as he observes various behaviours and reports on his tests. His work homes in on the stories of individual patients and expands to tell us not only what their experiences of illness reveal about how the human brain works, but how humans perceive the world we inhabit. Sacks follows in the footsteps of his patients as Richard Holmes follows in the footsteps of his writers.

His telling of the story of Dr P, a singer and music teacher, is part thriller, part achingly sad. Dr P's wife and friends had suggested he go to see a neurologist to have his strange mistakes investigated. At first Sacks is impressed by his patient's charming and intelligent personality, and can't see what the matter might be. After a physical examination he notices the man has not yet replaced his shoe.

He asks Dr P if he needs help putting on his shoes and sees that he is baffled by the question. Dr P looks down at his own foot and finally asks Sacks if his foot is his shoe. Sacks, in turn, is baffled:

> Did I miss-hear? Did he miss-see?…Was he joking?
> Was he mad? Was he blind? If this was one of his
> 'strange mistakes' it was the strangest mistake I had
> ever come across.

We are Sacks's colleagues or his students, his problems are our problems, and we are engrossed in helping the charming musical man who we discover can't even recognise that his wife's head is not his hat.

In an earlier book, *Awakenings*, published in 1973, Sacks tells the story of his use of L-DOPA on previously catatonic survivors of the 1917–1928 epidemic of 'sleepy sickness' or *encephalitis lethargica*. He dedicates the book to both Luria and to the English-born poet W. H. Auden.

Sacks met the New York–based Auden and another English poet, San Francisco–based Thom Gunn, when he was a young doctor working in the United States. He shared an interest in motorcycles with Gunn. When *Awakenings* was published, Gunn wrote to Sacks, revealing the dismay he had felt at the absence of empathy and affection in the young doctor when they had first met. Gunn was then in despair for Sacks as a human being. Was the change he detected when he read *Awakenings* due to drugs, analysis, falling in love or maturity? 'All of the above,' Sacks answered.

Sacks told me that these older poets taught him to look at disease, disorder and suffering in broader human terms, not only in narrow clinical or physiological terms. To examine the predicaments and plights of his patients and to write about their dignity and ingenuity as they coped with their lot.

And it is precisely this poetic approach that attracted me to Sacks's work, an approach that describes the subject matter from a multidimensional point of view, without losing the benefits of other kinds of scientific analyses.

'I think as a writer', says Sacks, 'one needs to bring out the passion and the purity of science, the excitement, the beauty, and the fact that science may provide the only way of observing and understanding immense phenomena that lie beyond the unaided senses—the causes of things, things which are below the surface, like atoms.'

But it goes both ways. Sacks also influenced the way Auden thought about the world. Auden dedicated his poem 'Talking to Myself' to Oliver Sacks, in which a human soul pleads with its body for a quick death when the time comes. Perhaps he was horrified by the thought of living for forty years after the onset of a debilitating illness, just as Sacks's 'sleepy sickness' patients had. And the poetic coda to the story of these patients was that most of them suffered terrible tics and other physical symptoms from the L-DOPA treatment, and sank back into their twilight world as if Sacks had never awakened them.

I admire the way Sacks has tackled his enormous project of writing on human perception, illness and the way we live with our afflictions. I love books that attempt big projects, focusing not just on an individual life, but on large, unlikely subjects. Like everything you might need to know about whales, exemplified by a natural history book that is also beautifully written, *Leviathan or, The Whale* by English writer Philip Hoare. Not only is it a love song to the whale, it celebrates the definitive whale novel, *Moby Dick*, and its author Herman Melville.

Philip Hoare had a fear of water, of what lay down below and he never really shook it. He only learned to swim when he was twenty-five. But from a very young age he was obsessed with whales, possibly coinciding with the 'Save the Whales' campaigns of the 1960s and 1970s, and he began to dream of them as heroic masters of the sea, which, given their size and the element in which they lived, were almost unknowable.

His obsession has taken on a romantic cast, sometimes

bordering on erotic. He says that he sought to discover why he felt haunted by the whale, by the forlorn expression on the beluga's face, by the orca's impotent fin, by the insistent images of these creatures in his head. 'Like Ishmael, I ran back to the sea, wary of what lay below, yet forever intrigued by it too.'

My first experience with sea creatures was when my father bought two goldfish from a man selling them from a bucket at the end of St Kilda pier. I was only three or four, and I wanted them as pets. The man put the fish in a plastic bag and I held it tightly all the way home. Of course my father hadn't thought ahead and we had no fishbowl, as my mother pointed out. The goldfish swam in the kitchen sink all afternoon, and I stood on a chair to watch them.

In the morning, I ran to the sink, which was empty. My father said he'd flushed the fish down the toilet. He shouted at me for crying, saying I was selfish for thinking my fish could live in the sink, when there were so many dishes to wash. I imagined the lives of my goldfish as they swam through the sewers and, I hoped, into the bay. And I thought of them when I went wading in the shallows at St Kilda beach. The girl who lived in the flat upstairs had a book called *The Water-Babies: A Fairy Tale for a Land-Baby* by the Reverend Charles Kingsley, in which Tom, a child chimney-sweep, falls into the water and drowns. I was fascinated by his resurrection as a water-baby. He could swim like a fish and breathe underwater.

The first sperm whale wasn't filmed underwater till the 1980s. We knew what the Earth looked like from outer space before we knew what a whale looked like underwater. There are species of beaked whale we know only from skeletons or beached remains. This is an immensely romantic idea, then, that a creature so embedded in our culture that it appears in the Bible can also be so mysterious.

And Herman Melville's novel *Moby Dick* is, for Hoare, a bible in itself, so imbued is it with *whaleness*—the sociology of the whalers, the politics of whaling—on almost every page. In the first chapter Melville describes the men who come down to the coast and look silently, longingly out at the sea, spellbound by the whaling life:

> Posted like silent sentinels all around the town, stand thousands upon thousands of mortal men fixed in ocean reveries. Some leaning against spiles; some seated upon the pier-heads; some looking over the bulwarks of ships from China; some high aloft in the rigging, as if striving to get a still better seaward peep.

Philip Hoare told me he studies his tiny edition of *Moby Dick* as he rides the London Tube as intently as the veiled woman next to him reads her Koran. He regrets that *Moby Dick* is set as a text for American high school students, who, at fifteen, won't be ready to take the book in. He thinks it has to be read chapter by chapter, without expectations that the narrative will tell one continuous story. There are a lot of digressions that he thinks can only make sense when one is ready for them. 'Wait until the moment is right,' he told me, 'the book will come up, and it will surface like a whale and it will present itself to you and it will say, "Read me," and at that point you will read that book and you won't put it down, and you will want to re-re-re-read it.'

Like the men in *Moby Dick*, most of us like to stare at the sea. Is it because that's where we all came from? Hoare is poetic too when he points out that whales started out on land and then went back to the sea, and as they still have to emerge from the water to breathe on the surface, perhaps they stare out at the land, to get a glimpse of us.

The romance and poetry of these ideas are undone with the realisation that if a whale were to reclaim its place on land it would be crushed by its own weight and die. In addition, whales are insulated by their blubber as they plunge to great depths where the temperature is very low. Blubber is highly efficient in retaining heat, but when a whale dies and it can no longer dissipate heat through its flukes and flippers, it can actually self-combust and will burn itself from the inside outwards. In arctic seas, whalers would slit open the animal and allow cold water in to prevent the creature burning in its own oil.

Hoare says the Inuit have a word for the fluke print of a whale—*qaala*—which is the calm circle of water that a whale (commonly a humpback) leaves as it dives. The Inuit believe that calm circle is a mirror into the whale's world and a mirror for the whale into our world. And isn't that what reading is for us, a mirror not only for our world but a place that gives it meaning?

What is the right moment to read a book? Is it when a book reflects the story of our own lives, so that we recognise the characters and what happens to them? Or is it before our own story takes the paths of characters? Do we read to show us how to avoid the events within? Has a book read at the right time saved any of us from certain doom?

We can't always choose the right moment to read a book. When Elizabeth Harrower's 1966 novel *The Watch Tower* was republished in 2012, after being out of print for many years, I read it for the first time. Now regarded as a classic, it is the story of two sisters who are abandoned by their mother after the death of their father. The setting is Sydney in the 1940s. Laura, the eldest, is forced to leave school for a job in a box factory, and, in order to look after her younger sister, Clare, she agrees to marry the owner of the factory. Felix controls the women with a mixture of purse-string-holding and hysteria. Laura becomes both afraid of Felix and complicit in the menace he creates, as she tries to bring Clare into their orbit.

I read *The Watch Tower* with a mixture of fascination and horror. It was impossible to put down. I saw several episodes in my own life mirrored in its pages. I wondered whether, had my mother read it and passed it on to me before she died, the course of my life might have changed. The answer is probably not. It's the kind of book that you only recognise in hindsight, such is the strength of blind optimism in the young. Or at least that was what I was like. Optimistic and fatalistic, I thought you had meekly to accept what life throws your way. Now I know better.

CHAPTER 10

# The aroma of faraway countries

In 1841 Ralph Waldo Emerson, who was trying to dissuade a friend from buying a Tuscan Villa, said, 'Let us not rove; let us sit at home with the cause...They who made England, Italy or Greece venerable in the imagination did so by sticking fast where they were. Travelling is a fool's paradise. The rage of travelling is a symptom of a deeper unsoundness affecting the whole intellectual action.'

But why not do both? Sitting at home reading the work of a trusted literary travelling companion can ready us for journeys to be undertaken, or can stand in for journeys never attempted.

The great travel writers Ibn Battuta and Marco Polo depended on their readers staying home and letting books take the place of their travels. These days we buy Lonely

Planet guidebooks and take ourselves off on our own adventures.

The finest travel books take me to places I might never visit myself. Travel is romance, and far-flung places are always exciting.

But who to trust and how to tell? The travel books that I've loved enough to keep at home are not those that necessarily give a tourist's flavour of a place—the sights to see, the food to eat—but those that bring a knowledge of the history, geography and language of the region together with a wisdom and humility to try to understand the journey. In many ways it's more important to like the narrator in travel books than it is to like the author of a novel. I'm happier to embark on the wings of imagination with a cad than to journey with a writer of non-fiction who comes across as ruthless or foolish or self-absorbed. Travel writers are my emissaries in the world, and I don't want them to be more unpleasant, insensitive or ill-informed than I am.

One of my favourite books is *The Faber Book of Reportage*. In it I first read of the 1709 rescue of Alexander Selkirk, a Scot, the son of a shoemaker, who had run away to sea and served under navigator, pirate and naturalist William Dampier. He'd had an argument with his betters about the seaworthiness of their vessel, the *Cinque Ports*, and tried to get others to mutiny. In 1704 he was punished for insubordination and left behind on an island off the coast of Chile where he lived by himself for more than four years. (The *Cinque Ports* later sank off the coast of Columbia.)

Woodes Rogers, the captain of the 'privateering' ship the *Duke*, reports on Selkirk's story. When Rogers picked him up he had some clothes and bedding, 'a firelock, some powder, bullets, and tobacco, a hatchet, a knife, a kettle, a Bible, some practical pieces, and his mathematical instruments and books'. Selkirk declared that he read, sang and prayed all the time he was alone, and that he was a better Christian for this. He had forgotten how to speak English, or perhaps how to speak to others, and Rogers says they had trouble understanding him. Selkirk declined their offer of alcohol and took a while to be able to share their food. Daniel Defoe must have read Rogers' account while researching his novel *Robinson Crusoe*.

Mama told me once that, after the war was over, she had forgotten how to speak Yiddish. She had spent four years living in fear that if she were to utter a single word in her first language it would give her away as an imposter. She was most worried that she might talk in her sleep while dreaming in Yiddish, and would be overheard by others who shared her barracks.

In another part of the Faber collection you can read the account of English artist B. R. Haydon, who sees the Elgin Marbles, the ancient Greek sculptures from the Acropolis, at Park Lane in London in 1808. His artist's eye details something that I would not have noticed:

> The first thing I fixed my eyes on was the wrist of
> a figure in one of the female groups, in which were
> visible, though in a feminine form, the radius and ulna.
> I was astonished, for I had never seen them hinted at in
> any female wrist in the antique. I darted my eye to the
> elbow, and saw the outer condyle visible affecting the
> shape as in nature. I saw that the arm was in repose
> and the soft parts in relaxation. That combination of
> nature and idea which I had felt was so much wanting
> for high art was here displayed to midday conviction.
> My heart beat!

And my heart beats too, to think of this private moment in 1808, felt and committed to paper, and then rediscovered and published in order for me to read more than two hundred year later, and to take pause, with the long dead.

The eyewitness to history is one exciting aspect of reportage, but in today's world, where everyone is a traveller and can blog to their heart's delight, how do we sift through the myriad offerings in order to find the writers we trust to be our emissaries as they take us to new adventures?

One of the best is Colin Thubron, whose last two books *Shadow of the Silk Road* and *To a Mountain in Tibet* were published in the years when it was my job to talk to writers, so I could judge for myself the kind of theoretical travel companion he might have been. Of course the thing about these writers is that they eschew all ideas of companions other than occasional ones they might meet on a journey. Travelling by yourself is really the only way to become dependent on the kindness or otherwise of locals who might take you into their homes and into their confidence. It is the only way for you to become like a stranger on a train, a safe person to confide in and never see again.

*Shadow of the Silk Road* connected the dots between subjects that have concerned and fascinated Thubron all his life—China, the former Soviet Union and Islam.

He started his journey in Xian, one of the first great capitals of China and the home of the terracotta warriors, sloped up into the far north-west, the Taklimakan Desert (which means in the local dialect 'you go in but you never come out'), crossed into Kyrgyzstan and Uzbekistan, then dropped down into Afghanistan, He travelled across into Iran to Mashhad and to Turkey, and finally to the sea port of Antioch. Thubron reached the little harbour, which was silted up, completely deserted, with a few fallen columns around it. In ancient times this was where the Silk Road ended.

'To follow the Silk Road is to follow a ghost,' he writes. 'It flows through the heart of Asia, but it has officially vanished, leaving behind it the pattern of its restlessness:

counterfeit borders, unmapped peoples.'

Fellow travel writer Pico Iyer once described Thubron as 'very much a traveller of the old school: educated at Eton, a descendent of John Dryden, and distinctly British and upper class in his diffidence and command of culture and language. A few generations ago, he might have been administering Khartoum.'

And he's right. Meeting Thubron when I interviewed him at the Edinburgh International Book Festival he was polite and self-effacing with a wistful, private sensibility and a vast knowledge of history, literature, politics and geography, which he imparted gently.

He's a man who travels lightly, with only a small rucksack. It was the same one he had on stage.

'I lay out everything I think I'm going to need,' he told me, 'and then ask myself whether I really need it, and the answer is almost always no, you need hardly anything. There's probably one change of clothes, fairly washable, there are language manuals, which means you've always got something to read, and notebooks. No camera; it renders you less suspicious if you have no camera. And that's about it. A very small medical kit. It's a lesson in how little you need.'

He had a satellite phone in order occasionally to call his elderly mother.

'I did once telephone and she answered suspiciously

quickly, and I was in North Afghanistan pretending to be somewhere else, and she said, "How are you?" and I said, "Oh I'm fine. I'm in..." I've forgotten where I pretended I was, somewhere rather safe, and I said, "How are you?" and she said, "I'm fine," and actually we were both lying. My mother, at the age of ninety-six, had gone ballooning, and the balloon had tipped over and bruised her sternum and she was lying in bed. And I was in Afghanistan pretending...so obviously this sort of lunacy runs in the family.'

When his mother died Thubron journeyed, like many Hindus and Buddhists who were making their pilgrimages, to Mount Kailash, in Tibet, the place Buddhists regard as the centre of the universe, near the source of the four great Indian rivers.

By then in his mid-sixties, Thubron employed Sherpas with a horse to carry his gear. In *To a Mountain in Tibet* he describes the desperately poor families he stayed with along the way, the food they eat and their hopes for the next generation. You trust his quiet approach, his knowledge and his openness in not coming to judgment too fast.

Thubron's romantic views of Tibet were stocked by a memory of reading James Hilton's 1933 novel *Lost Horizon* as a boy. I saw the film made in 1937 by Frank Capra on a tiny screen on a plane between Paris and Tokyo, imagining the scenes as I flew over the same territory. The story of the dashing writer–soldier–diplomat who rescues some westerners from China was my kind of tale of derring-do. The plane is hijacked, runs out of fuel and crashes in the Himalayas, but the group is rescued and taken to Shangri-la. Here you begin to hear the heavenly Hollywood tones of pure and mystical music, the kind they play in massage rooms at health spas. Everyone there is happy and the discontented westerners begin to lose all their troubles too.

Thubron imagined he would find in Tibet a government of seers, of prophets, and a pure sort of holy people, who would eventually be the salvation of the world. He was fired up by legends of monks who could levitate and fly, of lamas who could break rocks with their voices, and of the *lung-pa*, the wind men, who drifted over the landscape with their feet barely touching it. He was possessed by the idea that this land, in its extraordinary isolation, was a place of purity and promise, where all the poor things in human nature would in some way be redeemed.

But Thubron is not a proselytiser for Eastern ways. His reading taught him that the history of Tibet is dotted with wars. In the seventh and eighth centuries the Tibetans brought the great Chinese Tang dynasty to its knees. They sacked Xian. Their armies, wearing armour that was the finest in the world, reached the borders of Burma.

And even as late as the fifteenth century the great Tibetan monasteries weren't just places of worship and meditation, but also armed camps where monks from different sects would be at war with one another. Into the twentieth century the Dalai Lamas, if they weren't murdered in childhood, were sometimes complicit in violence. The idea of the Dalai Lama being a peaceable figure has arrived only with the present one.

Thubron told me about sky burial, the way the Tibetans dispose of their dead. 'The fact the ground is so hard, it's very hard to bury anyway,' he said, 'and they think that to place people in the soil is horrible, that we place our dead in the cold earth.' The 'sky master of burial' cuts up the corpse and pounds the bones, then feeds these morsels to vultures which assemble for the purpose.

'So the dead are completely consumed by vultures. And they believe that vultures are sacred; they say that you never see a dead one, that when they die they simply fly up towards the sun until the wind takes them apart. And so they, with the dead, simply disappear and that's their favourite way of disposing of corpses. And all this gives a kind of haunting feeling to us in the west about death and how you treat it.'

Reading about this is even more poignant because Thubron was walking to remember his dead—his parents, and his sister who died at just twenty-one—and in describing what happens to the corpses he must also be imagining the bodies of his own family.

If humility and an intelligent but highly informed light

touch are keys to good travel narratives, I was wonderfully served by the books of the late Ryszard Kapuściński, which are well represented on my shelves. He worked as a foreign correspondent for the Polish Press Agency, covering the African continent for more than forty years, during which twenty-seven revolutions and coups took place.

I met Kapuściński in Melbourne when I interviewed him at the writers festival and he invited me to stay in touch. The following year I travelled to Poland to make a radio documentary and he invited me to his home in Warsaw. He made me coffee and served me cake in his book-lined study upstairs, where he was deep in the research for a new book about Africa. Energetic and humble, hospitable and warm, like many foreign correspondents he seemed to be less comfortable in easy urban quarters than in the harsh terrain, writing about difficult politics far from his home.

Kapuściński wrote about the fall of Haile Selassie of Ethiopia, the collapse of Portuguese colonialism in Angola, the last days of the Shah of Persia, the end of the Soviet Union and in *The Shadow of the Sun* about his long love affair with Africa, which he described as an 'African fever'.

Reading Kapuściński throws you in to a strange world of metaphor and hyper-realism. He had a sharp eye for character, particularly of those in power and of those who fawn to them.

A few months after his death in 2007 at the age of seventy-four, the Polish edition of *Newsweek* exposed Kapuściński's collaboration with his nation's secret police between 1967 and 1972. But it's hard to see how his work abroad would have been permitted without such a liaison. It seems that nothing that Kapuściński reported to his would-be masters was of much interest to them. In fact his reports were carefully innocuous. He betrayed nobody. His books, especially *The Emperor: Downfall of an Autocrat* in which he recounted the fall of Haile Selassie, were read in Poland as veiled allegories of the Communist regime, and in 1981 his working credentials were withdrawn under Jaruzelski's martial law.

Kapuściński said, after the fall of communism, that his writing about the travesties of power was always understood by his Polish readers to be a coded commentary on what was happening at home.

The first time Kapuściński left on a foreign assignment, his editor gave him a copy of *The Histories*, Herodotus's witty, broadminded and cosmopolitan account of the ancient world. It became companion and guide to many of his travels. In 2004, he wrote *Travels with Herodotus* about these first trips, but it was only published in English after his death.

He took us to places where he never let us forget that we were strangers and his approach was to wonder at the ways that people found to make their lives. Here is Kapuściński on arriving in the heat of an African summer. Unlike the old journeys, which were slow and enabled the traveller to grow used to other climates and landscapes, the new arrival flies in and is plunged into the heat, the sounds and, above all, the smells:

> Perhaps he's had intimations of it. It is the scent that permeated Mr Kanzman's little shop, Colonial and Other Goods, on Perec Street in my hometown of Pinsk. Almonds, cloves, dates and cocoa. Vanilla and laurel leaves, oranges and bananas, cardamom and saffron. And Drohobych. The interiors of Bruno Schulz's cinnamon shops? Didn't their 'dimly lit, dark and solemn interiors' smell intensely of paints, lacquer, incense, the aroma of faraway countries and rare substances? Yet the actual smell of the tropics is somewhat different. We instantly recognise its weight, its sticky materiality. The smell makes us at once aware that we are at that point on earth where an exuberant and indefatigable nature labours, incessantly reproducing itself, spreading and blooming, even as it sickens, disintegrates, festers and decays.
>
> It is the smell of a sweating body and drying fish, of spoiling meat and roasting cassava, of fresh flowers and putrid algae—in short, of everything that is at once pleasant and irritating, that attracts and repels, seduces and disgusts.

Can you smell it, as I can, the fetid and the sweet, the rich and the pungent, the flinty and the smooth? Kapuściński is not only experiencing this at firsthand but he is imagining the realities described by the Jewish-Polish writer Bruno Schulz. All in two paragraphs.

He weaves history and philosophy together too, as he transports his reader to a world of complexities—amid the confusions and terrors of war he shows how difficult it can be to work out what is really going on. In his book on the fall of the Soviet Union, *Imperium*, he describes the lengths he went to in order to cover a 1990 conflict between Armenia and Azerbaijan. The fighting was being suppressed by the Soviets, and Kapuściński was finding it hard to get to Armenia to report.

His Armenian friends offer a solution—he will pretend to be an Aeroflot pilot. He dons the uniform and, with the cooperation of some Armenian pilots, he boards the plane, surrounded by crowds of angry passengers who have been waiting for a flight for days. After landing he gets into the back seat of the waiting car, and lies down, pretending to be dead drunk. It works. This little detail, like so many Kapuściński details, tells so much—in the Soviet Union a drunk pilot was completely normal.

In a 1994 discussion published by the *New York Review of Books*, Kapuściński said that during his life of travelling he developed a dislike for descriptions of people as politically on the right or the left, and for judging people according to their nationality:

> If someone tells me he is a left-wing Portuguese he tells me nothing about himself, because I still know nothing about the two characteristics which really count: what he is worth as a person and what sort of heart he has. Or in more flowery terms: whether he is clever and is a good human being. These are qualities which are of no interest to the policeman at the frontier who stretches out his hand for your passport, the only thing that matters to him is what passport you have, not whether you are a rogue or a genius. And that is what is so humiliating.

I'm deeply attracted to what I judge is the European sensibility in much of what Kapuściński writes, his use and understanding of history and philosophy and literature. And, in Australia, we are lucky to be able to rely on another such sensibility, in the work of writer and journalist Nicolas Rothwell. His imagination, clarity, seriousness of purpose and willingness to write about difficult landscapes, both social and geographic, make reading his prose a dreamy pleasure for me.

Born in New York, half-Czech and half-Australian, Rothwell is a polyglot polymath who has been based in northern Australia as correspondent for the *Australian* for many years. He has also worked extensively as a foreign correspondent for the paper, away from his beloved Darwin, which he calls 'the capital of the second chance'.

His books out of the north include *Wings of the Kite-Hawk*, *Another Country*, *The Red Highway* and *Journeys to the Interior*. Oxford-educated in classics, and with a sophisticated and diverse literary sensibility, Rothwell is an able and experienced traveller who can turn himself to bush mechanics and the remote Australian ethos when required:

> Geometry and disorder; law and lawlessness; a king tide of human classifying fervour, an ebbing away of pattern in nature itself; such is the north, where words multiply inside the wordlessness of the world, and where all human endeavours seem dwarfed from the moment of their undertaking.

Rothwell follows the trails of the explorers of remote Australia—Ludwig Leichhardt, Charles Sturt and Ernest Giles—of anthropologists and artists, of Aboriginal healers and leaders, of miners and archaeologists and travellers who want to lose themselves in the magical north. While his journalism is clear-eyed, his more discursive writing is romantic, seeking character and fate, exploring beauty and horror. Not strictly travel writing, his fictions and tales, essays and dreamscapes will take you on the kind of journey you could never make on your own.

Another person who became my friend and eccentric

travelling companion was the English writer Roger Deakin. I was introduced to him in a Mongolian yurt that had been erected in Charlotte Square in Edinburgh for the writers festival. He was a boyish man of sixty, lean and keen and laughing easily, with a head of longish grey curly hair. He was leaving for the station to catch the train for London, and asked if I knew his old friend Tony Barrell. Indeed I did know the late gifted radio documentary-maker, who was then a colleague. That was the end of the conversation. A few months later Roger Deakin's book was published in Australia and I interviewed him on the line from London.

He was a late bloomer who first made a career in advertising and then in documentary film-making. His celebrated first work was *Waterlog: A Swimmer's Journey through Britain*. After the break-up of a long relationship, Roger had the idea to swim his heart out beyond the confines of the ancient moat in which he swam lengths on his farm in Suffolk. He began to swim in and take notes about rivers and pools and seas and lakes throughout England:

> When you swim, you feel your body for what it mostly
> is—water—and it begins to move with the water
> around it. No wonder we feel such sympathy for
> beached whales; we are beached at birth ourselves.
> To swim is to experience how it was before you were
> born. Once in the water, you are immersed in an

intensely private world as you were in the womb. These amniotic waters are both utterly safe and yet terrifying, for at birth anything could go wrong, and you are assailed by all kinds of unknown forces over which you have no control.

Roger was sometimes called a 'nature writer', a term he disagreed with, as if you could hive off nature from life. His book is a physical and emotional geography of his beloved country and of his heart and soul. It's the best kind of travel writing. His last major work *Wildwood: A Journey through Trees* was finished four months before he died in 2007, of a brain tumour at sixty-three. This was another eccentric collection of notes about his meanderings through the forests of England, and through those as far afield as Kyrgyzstan and even Central Australia, on a trip we did together. As we travelled around I introduced him to people I had met on previous visits. At night, as we camped in dry creek beds, he would write notes in his journal, often till late. He'd call across to where I lay in my swag with entertaining interpretations of our experiences that day.

Once Roger tried to tell me that my fire-building technique (learned from Pitjanjatjara elders on a previous trip) would never do, and he showed me the proper British Boy Scout method of piling wood up. It didn't work, much to my pleasure. We went back to my method. A few days later he chastised me for pointing at a tree full of budgerigars, saying that no self-respecting naturalist would ever point at birds. It frightens them. He taught me to say 'budgerigars at three o'clock' if I must say anything at all. It was like travelling with a British public school headmaster crossed with one of the chaps from *Monty Python*.

Reading through *Waterlog* and *Wildwood* again, I am reminded how books can keep alive the voices of friends who have died, and make you smile again to remember the conversations and the days you have shared.

## CHAPTER II

# *A knife, a tobacco-pipe*

---

When I was a radio broadcaster specialising in writing, reading and ideas, one of the highlights of the work was the torrent of books that came pouring into my office from all over the world. Some of these managed to survive my treatment of close-reading, note-taking in margins and on the endpapers. I didn't offer them to colleagues or charities or to friends. They made it through to line the walls of my home. If I look at my shelves, certain patterns emerge and form themselves into collections. A library is a kind of autobiography of interests, of fads and life stages.

If novels are a way to explore fields of imagined places and characters, what are my books about exploration for? Why do I gravitate to travellers' tales? Where does my affection for explorers, particularly of polar regions, spring from?

I love a survival story. Especially in wild places. Preferably with detailed directions about what to pack, how to use one's wits to negotiate what the fates present, and how to improve one's fortunes.

I have a feeling it began with *Robinson Crusoe*. I'm sure I read one of the many abridged versions for children that followed the 1719 publication of Daniel Defoe's novel *The Life and Strange Surprizing Adventures of Robinson Crusoe, of York, Mariner: Who lived Eight and Twenty Years, all alone in an uninhabited Island on the Coast of America, near the Mouth of the Great River of Oroonoque; Having been cast on Shore by Shipwreck, wherein all the Men perished but himself. With An Account how he was at last as strangely delivered by Pirates.*

It wasn't a girl's book, and I was brought up in an era where the chasm between what was expected of girls and boys was wide. My library edition smelled of linoleum and sellotape. I imagined it might have smelled of boys.

So I decided to read the unabridged text. Robinson Crusoe goes to sea against the wishes of his father, becomes a slave, hunts for slaves and is eventually shipwrecked on an island, alone and with 'nothing about me but a knife, a tobacco-pipe, and a little tobacco in a box'.

This fascinated me, even more than the episode in which Crusoe discovers the ritual cannibalism of the visiting savages, or the footprint on the sand after he has been alone for many months. Man Friday is a welcome human companion, but the real question is, how do you survive on a desert island?

Crusoe begins to salvage all kinds of things from the shipwreck. And how clever he is in making use of such objects; he builds a home, a fort, and a ladder to pull up behind him as he secures his realm from attacks. He observes his discarded rat-eaten grains of dust which almost miraculously yield a few stalks of grain-bearing grasses, and with them he patiently cultivates his own stock of barley and corn from which he might finally in some long-distant future make himself some delicious bread.

Crusoe is aware that he knows nothing of threshing grain and making flour meal, of fashioning the loaf and baking the bread. He ponders on the many steps necessary to make this one article that he has until now taken for granted. It made me think of all those things that I have no idea how to make: soap, candles, matches—the list is long.

What would I do in Crusoe's situation? Would I ever have the luck, the perseverance and the patience not to gobble the grains at once, but to wait like the Little Red Hen, for the time when I could mill the grain and bake the bread?

I am reminded of Robinson Crusoe as I open my copy of Thor Heyerdahl's 1951 edition of *The Kon-Tiki Expedition: By Raft across the South Seas*. Who can fail to be seduced by the tone of Heyerdahl's (translated) prose, and his introduction, which takes place *in medias res*, in the middle of the story, exactly as the ancient poet Horace advised?

It is 1947 and Heyerdahl, with five fellow adventurers, is on a balsawood raft in the Pacific. He has just found 'seven flying fish on deck, one squid on the cabin roof, and one unknown fish in Torstein's sleeping bag'—a stroke of luck as Torstein Raaby is the cook this day. Now Heyerdahl is writing in his damp log-book on which is perched a green parrot, as one of his bearded companions is reading Goethe in the shadowy cabin beside him.

This is an irresistible entrée, which has all of the detail, character analysis and storytelling that you hope to find in a good novel.

Heyerdahl wanted to prove his theory of the foundation of Polynesian societies. His idea was essentially this: Peruvian Inca legends tell of a sun-king called Kon-Tiki who ruled over white people with beards who were called 'big-ears' because they elongated their ear lobes to reach their shoulders. These people built the giant statues in the Andes mountains before they were defeated by the Incas in battle and set off westwards on balsawood rafts.

On Rapa-Nui, or Easter Island, which lies on the route from Peru to Polynesia, the people tell a story of Tiki who, along with white 'long-ears' companions, came to the island from the east, skilled in the crafting of exactly the same statues that they erected here.

In Polynesia, the story told by people there was of Tiki, who had come across the sea from the east by raft, from a place called Pura from where the sun rose. Connecting the stories all made marvellous sense.

Heyerdahl's absurd derring-do, which luckily ends in no lives lost and a celebratory party on a tropical island, gives him heartening confirmation of his theory that sailors from Peru could have set out on rafts like his, carrying their Inca legends, and indeed settle Polynesia. However, since mitochondrial DNA analysis has been done on the populations of Polynesia, there is evidence that many of the islands were settled by Asian travellers, but there are South American gene-markers there too.

For many of my male friends, Thor Heyerdahl was a childhood hero, the embodiment of what the boy scouts were about, a modern Odysseus who built a raft and went voyaging on the high seas. For me, a girl with no brothers, no uncles and a distant relationship to my father, the six men on the raft were a fascinating glimpse into the mysteries of men.

One of the mysteries is what Heyerdahl and his companions packed for the voyage. I was inevitably curious about this. Heyerdahl tells us that Erik Hesselberg had stowed several rolls of drawing paper and a guitar. His allocated box was so full that he had to put his socks in Raaby's box. Bengt Danielsson's box held nothing but books, all seventy-three of which were on sociology and ethnology. My sympathies were with Bengt, as I too had developed a passion for books of this kind.

Margaret Mead's 1928 *Coming of Age in Samoa* and later her *Growing Up in New Guinea* were two of the first ethnographies that intrigued me, and it turns out that they engaged a generation of people who were looking for different ways to understand the changes in the sexual mores of the west. Mead described a Samoan society with a comparatively relaxed attitude to adolescent sexuality, and other Pacific communities where warfare was not the dominant trope.

But it was Colin Turnbull's work *The Mountain People*, about the Ik of Uganda, that moved me to take a few anthropology subjects at university when I found it hard to continue an interest in scientific research while pregnant and with a toddler at home. It was 1977. My father had left my mother during her final illness to live with a woman he subsequently married, leaving me and my sister to care for Mama till she died ten months later.

*The Mountain People* was a truly shocking study of a group in extremis, the survivors of a famine in which parents seemed not to care for their families, adults took food from the mouths of children, and treated the dying with cruelty. The Ik were described as spies and double-dealers in their relations with other tribes. How interesting this field of study seemed!

My first sighting of my anthropology lecturer confirmed that I was in the right place. It's only now that I see why I was so convinced that the study of human behaviour in small-scale societies was for me. I was eight months pregnant and twenty-three, and he was perhaps just fifty and built like Ernest Hemingway, barrel-chested, bearded, pipe-smoking and, most importantly, sporting a knife in a scabbard hanging off his belt—like Defoe's Crusoe he also had nothing about him 'but a knife, a tobacco-pipe, and a little tobacco in a box'.

His command of many languages, African and European, ancient and modern, was impressive enough, but when I learned that he had been a district officer in Botswana before he completed his PhD I just knew that if ever I found myself in a tough and remote situation he was the man who would be able to shoot an elephant, divine water, gather appropriate berries and lead me home.

Why I thought that my life then in all its settled suburban glory was in danger of going so far off the rails that I might be threatened with an elephant stampede, I do not know. Within a couple of years I became decoupled from my husband, but it was nothing to do with my lecturer, who remained blissfully ignorant of my romantic projections.

But he did point out some other romantic projections that I may have been nurturing, when I mentioned Colin Turnbull's work. 'Ah, the sick Ik,' he said. He seemed not to be as impressed as I was. By 1985 Turnbull's work was to be challenged by anthropologists who revisited the Ik and claimed that Turnbull had been speaking to informants who were not fluent in Ik and sometimes not even Ik, and had been in error in his analysis of their hunting, gathering and farming practices. If the Ik had indeed been spies and double-dealers, their position among their neighbours would have been subject to bloody reprisals long ago, it was claimed. Turnbull was accused of projecting his own antisocial feelings onto the Ik.

My faith in ethnography was shaken even further when I heard Margaret Mead's reputation take a beating in a paper by Derek Freeman, a professor at the Australian National University, who revealed that he had revisited her field sites in Samoa and found a very different set of circumstances there. In his 1983 book *Margaret Mead and Samoa: The Making and Unmaking of an Anthropological Myth* he claimed that Mead, who wrote about casual sex among teenagers in Samoa, for example, had been told what she wanted to hear by her teenage informants. A huge international argument ensued—Mead was dead by then and couldn't defend herself—and after some years it emerged that the Samoans themselves thought that both anthropologists had got them wrong.

I was in New Zealand when I heard Freeman speak at a scientific congress. I remember going to a *hangi*, a traditional pit-based pig barbecue party, where I met Reo Fortune, Margaret Mead's second husband, who was himself a New Zealander but by then he was rather elderly and somewhat inebriated. I was too star-struck to make any sensible conversation, apart from identifying him as a former Mr Mead. As he had been so since 1935 he was understandably less than interested.

All of them are dead now, but this was the time when my taste for mediated accounts of traditional peoples in remote places began to be replaced by firsthand accounts and the journals of explorers. I wanted to read of voyages, not merely travels. And as a nervous traveller, who fights against the panic of what will happen if I don't pack exactly what I need (while desperate not to take too much), nothing impressed me more than the planning required for some of the legendary polar expeditions.

I had become attracted to snowy stories. I always had a romantic vision of the sledge and the dogs pulling it, and I now realise this derived from seeing the film of *Dr Zhivago* with my mother. I wanted more than anything to be Julie Christie as the brave and beautiful Lara, wrapped in furs and pulled through the snow by leaping dogs with an adoring Omar Sharif (minus the moustache) by my side.

Early in my career as a literary journalist, I fell upon the biography of Fridtjof Nansen. Born in the middle of the nineteenth century, he was the father of modern polar exploration, a Norwegian polymath who was a central-nervous-system biologist, an oceanographer, a historian and a diplomat. He ended his career working for the League of Nations as High Commissioner for Refugees and for the Repatriation of Prisoners of War.

Using his diaries and letters, Nansen's biographer Roland Huntford paints a picture of a moody, dogged man, who had to invent many things before he could undertake his voyages across Greenland or towards the North Pole. In Nansen's own 1897 account of his voyage, *Farthest North: Being the Record of a Voyage of Exploration of the Ship 'Fram' 1893–96* he declares, 'But the spirit of mankind will never rest till every spot of these regions has been trodden by the foot of man, till every enigma has been solved.'

Nansen devoted himself to learning how Eskimos lived, and in doing so adopted their methodology for dog sledding. He modified a technique for cross-country skiing for his journey across Greenland (no one thought he would survive). He designed not only his ship, which he called the *Fram*, but a light-weight sledge, the clothing his expeditioners needed for trekking, sleeping bags and even a spirit stove. The pure alcohol needed to run it was also drinkable, and Nansen was concerned that his party not debauch themselves (he frowned at their carousing even on their last night in port) so he turned it into methylated spirits. He then took absolute control by cooking everything himself. His diaries show him to be driven by his ambitions and tormented by his inability to achieve things to the level he required.

He could be difficult and gloomy ('sad even when enthusiastic, mirthless even when eager', according to an account by Norwegian businessman Jonas Lied) and yet he convinced an assortment of men to follow him on trips that sometimes lasted years. He was passionate about preparation and about the need for careful scientific observations. In turn he studied accounts of the failures of his predecessors, and disapproved of the rush in which they had planned and equipped their trips. His took nine years in the conceptual framing and three years to plan.

So strong was the pull of my romantic *Dr Zhivago* vision, and so deep was my admiration for the manly arts of Nansen, that in my mid-forties I found myself behind a team of seven Alaskan huskies at South River, in the Algonquin State Park, three hours north of Toronto in Canada.

There I met Hosea, a small but determined little dog that led the team and taught me lessons about bravery, humour and sheer pluck, and that appearances are not all they seem. That even the most courageous of us have foibles that make us, well, vulnerable.

Preparing in Australia for my expedition I had anxiously filled out my list of extreme polar clothing and nifty little headlights and a Swiss army knife and many pairs of socks and gloves and something called a neck protector, while the mercury outside climbed to 40 °C.

My guide was a 25-year-old man full of Canadian niceness, which came in handy later when I spent the whole of the first day's travels flinging either myself or him out of the speeding sled.

It turned out there wasn't very much at all between the driver and the snow, but I was assured that the light-framed white ash sled, lashed together with ropes to make it flexible, was strong and functional. At the front there was a structure like a bullbar to deflect small brush trees along the trails. Between the two runners was the brake—a metal arrangement, which you either pressed on slowly or jumped on with all your weight, depending on how quickly you wanted to stop. The only other controls were to shout directions to the dogs, and to grip the back of the sled at all times. When you needed to stop, the sled had a snow-hook, like an anchor, and after you tipped the sled on its side you wrapped the hook around a tree so the dogs didn't lunge the sled away and abandon you.

I found it easy to imagine watching the sled team rushing off into the distance because I had forgotten to secure the snow-hook. But I had read other accounts of snowy landscapes in order to pick up invaluable hints for survival. Instructive was John McPhee, the *New Yorker* essayist and adventurer, who reported in his book *Coming into the Country* a meeting with Leon Crane, who had survived a plane crash in the Alaskan wilderness and then emerged long after people had given him up for dead.

When Crane crashed he was wearing 'a hooded down jacket, a sweater, winter underwear, two pairs of trousers, two pairs of socks, and felt-lined mukluks.' Mukluks? No one said I needed these high soft-soled sealskin boots. Where was I going to get a seal at this late stage?

Crane had two books of matches and a scout knife. He used the matches and a letter from his father to light a fire. His cut his hands from tearing at spruce boughs, and it was his parachute that kept him alive. 'It was twenty-eight feet in diameter, and he wound it around him so that he was the centre of a great cocoon.' I had neglected to take a sheaf of letters from my father and hadn't seen a parachute in any of my shopping expeditions. And could I take matches and a knife on the plane from Australia?

My guide taught me the signals for stopping and starting ('Let's go!' and 'Whoa!'), which, if you are not careful to speak with a Canadian twang, and growl low and high, can sound the same.

The lead dogs had to be harnessed first and clipped at the head of the mainline. Then the point dogs in the middle section, and the wheel dogs at the back. The guide whispered that the lead dogs were the smartest, his hushed tones implying that the wheel dogs would be offended if they knew we were speaking like this. But the truth is that the wheel dogs were used to following the leaders, and had a tendency to get themselves all mixed up and the line tangled if they couldn't see little Hosea, our unprepossessing black, white and cream lead dog. When they got the line tangled they were more likely to chew it, which was akin to doing something terrible to your car's universal joint.

We were loaded and with a 'Ready—let's go!' we were off along the frozen lanes. I felt the light sled with its tongue-in-groove construction giving play to the bumps and speed traps on the way.

Soon we were off across a white lake, and then followed smaller snowy trails through the forest. It was bitterly cold on the sled and I gave silent thanks for my thermal layer, covered by my polartec layer covered with Gore-Tex. Suddenly I could see the point of a neck protector.

We said 'get ahead' when the line was slacking and 'good dogs—let's work!' when we came to a hill. This was where the passenger had to jump off the sled and run up the hill behind it. The dogs had been pulling the weight of two people, their food, our food, our clothes and general camping gear. If you were driving, you did the same as the passenger, but hung on to the back of the sled. Sometimes you could get away with a scooter-like move with one leg, but you had to be ready to fix the leg firmly on the runners as the dogs reached the top and took off down the other side.

After a few hours the runners iced over, which made the whole procedure quite slippery and as I leaned left and right, trying to balance the sled around corners, I often lost my footing. Once, flung into a snow bank, I was unable to get a grip and turn over. I thought of Kafka's beetle in *Metamorphosis* and began the laughing that sounds like crying to those in the world above the snowy pit.

Hosea was a crab-runner—his left shoulder faced forward because of a congenital hip problem common in canines. Alaskan huskies are quite small, the size of a blue heeler. They are the marathon runners of dogs, but I was surprised at their lack of physical presence, as they dragged the load through the landscape.

I thought of the Norwegian Roald Amundsen, who in 1911 reached the South Pole five weeks earlier than the English explorer Robert Scott. The Englishman relied on technology and took tractors, which broke down, while Amundsen had a team of trusty dogs that got him to his destination, and fed him on the way back. In his 1912 book *The South Pole: An Account of the Norwegian Antarctic Expedition in the* Fram*, 1910–1912* Amundsen is practical in his descriptions of slaughtering the weaker dogs and feeding the stronger ones on their bodies. And if the men hankered after fresh meat they helped themselves to a slice of dog which, according to Amundsen, tasted as good as the best beef. The dogs, he says, ate everything except the teeth, but on a really hard day these disappeared as well.

Hosea, however, running his heart out at the head of the team, did not look particularly appetising to me.

The skittishness and moodiness of the dogs gave way to high spirits as we neared the campsite. We stopped for some of the dogs to relieve themselves, but Spot, a wheel dog, had perfected the method of defecating while running.

When we reached the campsite, we were wet from the inside out, but all the dogs had to be unharnessed and taken over to a hitching area where they were chained up for the night. They were each watered and fed and given a palette of straw, which they moved about like a little nest, before they lay down, with their noses under their tails. Although Hosea was a brave team leader, he was, at the end of a day's work, afraid of putting his head in a bucket to drink the warm soupy water. He required a bowl, or he refused entirely. Every hero, it seemed, had his weak points. Granite and Harry might have been big stupid wheel dogs, but they were smart enough to know that there were gems of food scraps at the bottom of the bucket and they both kicked it over to find them. I learned to water them last.

After two nights out we were all ready for the trip home. Spot almost ran on his hind legs as I delivered him back to the yard. There he was, among two hundred and fifty other dogs, while I was almost hypothermic with cold and tiredness. I said goodbye to the dogs and thanked them for their work. But I saved a special pat for Hosea, the little dog that could.

Fridtjof Nansen writes of his first, rather lame, attempts at driving a sledge with ten dogs. Sitting in the sledge he was hijacked when his team spied a strange dog at the edge of the camp. They fell over each other in a rush to attack the animal, biting and tearing at it, drawing blood while the strange dog yelped. Nansen threw himself on the pack, bellowing. 'Dog-driving, at any rate to begin with,' he reflected, 'requires much patience.'

How much less sanguine I would have been on that Canadian dog-sledding trip if I had read Nansen's account of the dogs before I read Amundsen. When times were happy and the hard work was still to come, the dogs were joyous, rolling in the snow, 'a cheerful sight'. Later, as things got harder, Nansen and his partner Hjalmar Johansen had to strangle a number of the dogs and butcher them in order to feed the survivors.

This was the origin of the phrase 'dog eat dog'. The behaviour of the dogs, as they 'hounded' other weaker animals and set upon them in a pack, underlined the stark reality of what survival really means. As they neared the next part of the trip, a journey by kayak, Nansen and Johansen had to make a hard decision. They had no room for the dogs. But they had become so fond of the last two that they couldn't bear to strangle them. They used two precious cartridges instead. In a gesture of mutual compassion, Nansen shot Johansen's dog and Johansen shot his.

## CHAPTER 12

# The great white desert

When my parents took my sister and me for a walk to the kiosk at the end of St Kilda pier, I looked forward to the vanilla ice cream in a cone that was our reward for good behaviour. My father told us that ice cream came from the South Pole, which he said he could just see over the horizon. I've always enjoyed the idea that the southerly wind whipping across Port Phillip Bay blew directly from the pole, which I still hope to visit one day.

But I have visited Robert Scott's ship *Discovery*, which took him to the Antarctic for the first time in 1901, at Dundee on the east coast of Scotland. I found it completely absorbing for the few hours it took to examine every part of the exhibition—which covers both Scott's Discovery and Terra Nova expeditions—to press every button, and to listen to every soundscape of the wind and the snow. You can go aboard the ship and see the crested expedition crockery and the brass bars around the dining table, which stopped it smashing off the surface in a storm. Scott imposed Royal Navy procedures: officers ate separately from the men. While they were frozen in ice for two years in Antarctica they kept up an officers' mess, officers' clubs and officers' quarters. The officers had certain privileged liquors and alcohol; they had cigars while the men had cigarettes. A class distinction ran through the entire expedition.

In Dundee I saw the thin leather clothing that men wore in freezing conditions—today no self-respecting bikie would wear such little protection in temperate weather. I read the menu for 22 June 1903 (turtle soup, halibut cutlets, plum pudding and jellies) and read about the harmonium presented to the expeditioners by the people of Christchurch. A copy of *Gulliver's Travels* is on display, a present from Sir Clements Markham, who launched Scott's career.

Scott's journal from the Terra Nova expedition is full of his yearning for adventure, for knowledge. Proud of being English, he is in pursuit of 'wild doings in wild countries'. His men spend their days in readiness for their last strike out for the pole, the Southern Journey, taking turns giving lectures on their specialities—Lawrence Oates on feeding the horses, Edward Wilson on sketching, Edward Atkinson on parasitology, Frank Debenham on volcanoes and Charles Wright on ice problems.

In Antarctica Scott lists his impressions of the landscape, which dwarfs his camp in the vast whiteness. They make a kind of poetry:

*Impressions*

The seductive folds of the sleeping-bag.

The hiss of the primus and the fragrant steam of the cooker issuing from the tent ventilator.

The small green tent and the great white road.

The whine of a dog and the neigh of our steeds.

The driving cloud of powdered snow.

The crunch of footsteps which break the surface crust.

The wind blown furrows.

The blue arch beneath the smoky cloud.

The crisp ring of the ponies' hoofs and the swish of the following sledge.

The droning conversation of the march as driver encourages or chides his horse.

The patter of dog pads.

The gentle flutter of our canvas shelter.

Its deep booming sound under the full force of a blizzard.

The drift snow like finest flour penetrating every hole and corner—flickering up beneath one's head covering, pricking sharply as a sand blast.

The sun with blurred image peeping shyly through the
wreathing drift giving pale shadowless light.

The eternal silence of the great white desert. Cloudy
columns of snow drift advancing from the south, pale
yellow wraiths, heralding the coming storm, blotting
out one by one the sharp-cut lines of the land.

The blizzard, Nature's protest—the crevasse, Nature's
pitfall—that grim trap for the unwary—no hunter
could conceal his snare so perfectly—the light
rippled snow bridge gives no hint or sign of the
hidden danger, its position unguessable till man
or beast is floundering, clawing and struggling for
foothold on the brink.

The vast silence broken only by the mellow sounds of
the marching column.

Another account of Scott's second expedition, Apsley
Cherry-Garrard's *The Worst Journey in the World*, was published in 1922. It starts with much charm:

Polar exploration is at once the cleanest and most
isolated way of having a bad time which has been
devised. It is the only form of adventure in which you
put on your clothes at Michaelmas and keep them on
until Christmas, and, save for a layer of the natural
grease of the body, find them as clean as though they
were new. It is more lonely than London, more secluded
than any monastery, and the post comes but once a

year. As men will compare the hardships of France,
Palestine, or Mesopotamia, so it would be interesting to
contrast the rival claims of the Antarctic as a medium
of discomfort.

In July 1911 Cherry-Garrard set out from the main party
with Henry 'Birdie' Bowers and Edward Wilson, on their
'Winter Journey' to obtain emperor penguin embryos
to study. The Discovery expedition had been the first to
find emperor penguin rookeries. The flightless birds were
thought to be part of the evolutionary march from reptiles
to birds. The emperor penguin bred in the middle of winter, unlike any other bird, in the middle of the worst season
in the most desolate part of the planet.

The mystery was why this was the case when the temperature was seventy degrees below zero and the blizzards
didn't let up, and the chicks had to balance on the feet of
the mother or father, cuddling against a bald patch on the
parent's breast. Cherry-Garrard was fascinated by the penguins' child-rearing practices:

> And when at last he simply must go and eat something
> in the open leads nearby, he just puts the child down
> on the ice, and twenty chickless Emperors rush to pick
> it up. And they fight over it, and so tear it that
> sometimes it will die. And, if it can, it will crawl into
> any ice-crack to escape from so much kindness, and
> there it will freeze.

On an earlier expedition, they reported that the emperor chick was still without feathers at the beginning of January. If the same egg had been laid in summer, it would have been without protection the following winter. The emperor penguin has to put up with nesting hardships 'because his children insist on developing so slowly, very much as we are tied in our human relationships for the same reason. It is of interest that such a primitive bird should have so long a childhood.'

The youngest member of Scott's group, Cherry-Garrard was nearly blind without his glasses, which he had to remove while sledding. He had little scientific training and had never been to the Antarctic. The three men embarked on their journey in total darkness with temperatures down to seventy-five-below, the coldest temperature recorded up to that time. They trekked for one hundred and twenty kilometres in their thin gabardine outfits, manhauling the sleds, which were loaded with three-quarters of a tonne of research equipment and their supplies. The idea was to obtain the fresh penguin embryos and dissect them in a laboratory they were going to construct. They planned to build a stone hut on a rocky outcrop some kilometres up Mount Terror, a structure they could heat and work in. As if this were not hard enough, they decided to use this trek to test the perfect diet for the polar attempt the next summer, so they divided up the types of food—biscuits, pemmican and butter—and each ate a different proportion of fats to protein to carbohydrates. It was so cold their teeth chattered until some of them shattered.

After five weeks they finally brought three emperor penguin eggs back to the expedition camp. They had collected five, but two broke on the way from the rookery to the hut. They examined the insides of these eggs, as well as those smashed and discarded eggs they had seen at the rookery.

From their base camp, Scott, Wilson, Bowers and Oates set out on the 'Southern Journey' to the pole. As the months passed, Scott's poetic impressions of the camp had turned to a loss of confidence in his use of horses and sledges and his journal entries became restrained. He realises he had been too confident in his strategy of using horses and motor sledges. His cheery tone fades once he understands that the Norwegian explorer Roald Amundsen has got to the pole first, and left him a letter:

> Dear Captain Scott—As you probably are the first to reach this area after us, I will ask you to kindly forward this letter to King Haakon VII. If you can use any of the articles left in the tent please do not hesitate to do so. The sledge left outside may be of use to you. With kind regards I wish you a safe return.
>
> Yours truly,
>
> Roald Amundsen

What did Amundsen mean about the letter for the King of Norway? Was it a snide reference to Scott being his servant, now that he had been bested at the pole? Scott maintained he was on a scientific expedition rather than a race, and indeed the doomed men hauled back thirty-two pounds of geological specimens with them for the cause of science, but how did he take the news of coming second?

On their return journey the weather turned worse and the men faltered with illness and lack of provisions. I adore these shivering stories of men pitted against the elements because they are ripe with tragedy, bravery and the truth of human nature under extremes of pressure. They are romantic too, in the pursuit of such an abstract goal. There was nothing to see at the South Pole to distinguish it from any other part of the polar plateau. They sacrificed all for an idea.

The best-known story of the Southern Journey is that of Captain Lawrence Oates. 'I am just going outside and may be some time,' Oates said to the others on the morning of 16 March 1912, his parting words to the men he wanted to save, after accepting that he was no longer able to walk. The three he left behind—Scott, Wilson and Bowers—died a couple of weeks later, only a few kilometres short of their goal. Imagine the scene of Scott writing till the last, scrawling messages to the men's families and pleas for the care of his wife and child.

Scott's mentor, Sir Clements Markham, writes in his introduction to *Scott's Last Expedition: The Journals* that the explorer, with the bodies of his men beside him, wrote until the pencil dropped from his frozen hand. His last words were to reassure Markham that he should feel no guilt for sending the men to their deaths, saying he never regretted being in command of the expedition.

Reading Amundsen's *The South Pole* I'm aware that his proud account of his success at reaching the pole was written in Brisbane in the months after his return. He was to embark on a series of worldwide lectures, and he was buoyed by his sense that he had the right approach, the right equipment and perhaps the right nationality to have succeeded. Fridtjof Nansen himself wrote an introduction to Amundsen's book and pointed out that the methods and means that brought him success were those of the nomads who had lived and journeyed in harsh northern polar conditions for thousands of years, rather than those invented in the present day. He praised the meticulous planning and execution of the expedition: 'It is the man that matters, here as everywhere.'

I wondered if Amundsen and Nansen would have adopted such a tone—proud and challenging the follies of the other party—if they had known that the bodies of Scott and his companions lay dead in the ice, Scott's journal frozen to his very chest? When the world learned of their fate, and the bodies were found in late 1912, opinion turned against the Norwegians, and Amundsen was accused of being underhanded by switching his expedition from the North Pole to the South Pole without telling anyone until he was well on the way.

So what happened to the three penguin eggs for which Cherry-Garrard, Edward Wilson and Birdie Bowers had risked their lives in such atrocious conditions? Cherry-Garrard arrived at the Natural History Museum in London in 1913, four years after the expedition had set out, the sole survivor of the Winter Journey—he had not been in the party for the Southern Journey. His reception was deeply disappointing. The egg specimens were no longer interesting to the scientists there, as the theory about the importance of emperor penguin embryology to the evolution of birds had begun to be discredited. The visit is reported by Cherry-Garrard with humour:

> I resort to Mr. Brown, who ushers me into the presence of the Chief Custodian, a man of scientific aspect, with two manners: one, affably courteous, for a Person of Importance (I guess a Naturalist Rothschild at least) with whom he is conversing, and the other, extraordinarily offensive even for an official man of science, for myself.
>
> I announce myself with becoming modesty as the bearer of the penguins' eggs, and proffer them. The

Chief Custodian takes them into custody without a word of thanks, and turns to the Person of Importance to discuss them. I wait. The temperature of my blood rises. The conversation proceeds for what seems to me a considerable period...Feeling that to persist in overhearing their conversation would be an indelicacy, the Heroic Explorer politely leaves the room, and establishes himself on a chair in a gloomy passage outside, where he wiles away the time by rehearsing in his imagination how he will tell off the Chief Custodian when the Person of Importance retires. But this the Person of Importance shows no sign of doing, and the Explorer's thoughts and intentions become darker and darker. As the day wears on, minor officials, passing to and from the Presence, look at him doubtfully and ask his business. The reply is always the same, 'I am waiting for a receipt for some penguins' eggs.' At last it becomes clear from the Explorer's expression that what he is really waiting for is not to take a receipt but to commit murder.

But the tone and humour of the account belies the truth—Apsley Cherry-Garrard was in the search party that found the bodies of Scott, Bowers and Wilson. When he returned from the pole he suffered long and serious mental illness that we might today ascribe to post-traumatic stress disorder. He worried that he should have been able to do something, anything, to save Scott and the others. His later account was written under the guidance of his neighbour George Bernard Shaw.

Cherry-Garrard's biographer Sara Wheeler paints a picture of a passionate but shy man, who at fifty courted his twenty-year-old bride-to-be, Angela Turner, by giving her a stone on a beach. 'Years later,' writes Wheeler, 'when she had become an Antarctic expert, Angela discovered that the courtship ritual of the penguin centres around stone-giving, stones being a vital commodity for the construction of the nest.'

Not all the Antarctic adventures ended quite as tragically. Ernest Shackleton was on the *Discovery* with Scott, but was sent home unwell in the middle of the expedition, which he felt to be a personal failure. He certainly made up for it later, and his memoir *South* tells of another journey that didn't strictly succeed in its aims, but became a fantastic story of endurance and wit and great leadership. In 1914, on the *Endurance*, he set out to cross the Antarctic continent from sea to sea, via the pole. On another ship, the SY *Aurora*, the Ross Sea party was tasked with providing supply depots to enable the main party's survival. But the *Endurance* was trapped in pack-ice and crushed before the men could begin their cross-continental journey. After adventures on ice floes, Shackleton's party landed on remote Elephant Island. He left the crew there, sheltering under two upturned boats, while a small group struck out for South Georgia, from where he knew help was available from those at the whaling stations fifty kilometres from the landing point.

I love the way Shackleton sets out the parameters of the problems he has to solve, and the strategies he will use to solve them. To give poor Scott his due, his notes were made under terrible conditions, while Shackleton wrote and published his book a few years after his return. Shackleton, who had been a journalist and public lecturer, is a more engaging writer than Scott.

There is so much to learn from Shackleton's book. He gives you an ice education and includes an ice glossary: pancake ice, hummocky floes, growlers, to name a few. You learn that old seal bones can be dug up and stewed down in sea water to eat when things get tough. That blubber is good for making lamps and for eating. One of the last things Shackleton removed from the sinking *Endurance* was a banjo. The men left on Elephant Island had a concert every Saturday night, each singing a song about another member of the party.

I'm taking his book with me if ever I voyage south of Tasmania, as much for the recipes for seal blubber as the adventure. Shackleton took to rearranging the weekly menu, as the number of permutations of how to cook seal meat was decidedly limited. The men didn't know what to expect and this was useful in order to surprise them.

And their joy at being rescued was palpable too. When Shackleton reached the whaling station with two men, their first night in a room with an electric light and warm, soft beds was so comfortable that he says they were unable to sleep. He immediately arranged for the retrieval of the men who were waiting at the landing place at South Georgia as well as those who had waited on Elephant Island for four and half months by the time they were rescued. Three men of the Ross Sea party had died.

After this ordeal, Shackleton mounted another expedition in 1921, but died of a heart attack while his ship was moored in preparation. He was buried at Grytviken in South Georgia, at rest at last.

## CHAPTER 13

# *This deep darkness of night*

Some people pack books about journeys that other people have taken when they themselves are travelling. Others can't imagine doing this. There are several schools of thought. Will reading about another journey take away from your own experience of it? Or will discovering the differences between someone else's journey and your own heighten your experience? Or, if you want to have your own experience of the place, perhaps a novel that takes you to an utterly different place is best.

My adored polar explorers were the best prepared of men. I'm always intrigued to know how they passed the time on expeditions, and what they read.

Apsley Cherry-Garrard praised the usefulness of modern novels. 'You often want the book which you read for half an hour before you go to sleep at Winter Quarters to take you into the frivolous fripperies of modern social life which you may not know and may never wish to know, but which it is often pleasant to read about, and never so much so as when its charms are so remote as to be entirely tantalising.'

He admired the books of George Bernard Shaw, H. G. Wells and Henrik Ibsen for their ability to fire discussions of ideas among the men. He reports that Scott took some Browning poetry on the polar journey, but Cherry-Garrard only saw him reading it once. On the other hand, Scott was glad he'd had the foresight to take Darwin's *The Origin of Species* on their first southern journey.

Cherry-Garrard also praised the usefulness of poetry for the expeditioner:

> It gave one something to learn by heart and repeat during the blank hours of the daily march, when the idle mind is all too apt to think of food in times of hunger, or possibly of purely imaginary grievances, which may become distorted into real foundations of discord under the abnormal strain of living for months in the unrelieved company of three other men.

Cherry-Garrard reports that when they met their geological group near the beginning of their journey, they were excited about the additional books that they could now share:

Books of reference were constantly in demand to settle disputes. Such books as the *Times Atlas*, a good encyclopaedia and even a Latin Dictionary are invaluable to such expeditions for this purpose. To them I would add *Who's Who*.

From odd corners we unearthed some Contemporary Reviews, the *Girls' Own Paper* and the *Family Herald*, all of ten years ago! We also found encased in ice an incomplete copy of Stanley Weyman's *My Lady Rotha*; it was carefully thawed out and read by everybody, and the excitement was increased by the fact that the end of the book was missing.

While the *Endurance* became trapped and nine months later was crushed by ice and sank beneath the crust, the men had a portion of the *Encyclopaedia Britannica* (with descriptions of American towns, and complete biographies of every American statesman since George Washington), a few books on Antarctic exploration, Browning's poems and Coleridge's *The Rime of the Ancient Mariner*.

One man had a 'small penny cookery book' and 'from this he would read out one recipe each night, so as to make them last.' The men were obsessed with puddings (such as spotted dog) and with doughnuts and one of them 'eulogises Scotch shortbread'.

Travel writer Paul Theroux recommends taking a novel on a journey, one that has nothing to do with the place you are in. He uses fiction to rest his mind, as a way of retreating from the demands of a new place with its unfamiliar ways. He argues that we're never more sure of the people we're with than when we're reading a novel. We know the characters more intimately than our friends, or our family. We might even know them better than we know ourselves.

Theroux told me that if the novel you are reading is set in the country that you're visiting—let's say you're in India, reading *A Passage to India* by E. M. Forster—then you will be constantly reminded that the story takes place in 1922, creating a cognitive dissonance between the India of the novel and the India that you are experiencing. But if you're reading *Madame Bovary* in India then you will be in her world: she is committing adultery, she owes money, she is lying to her husband, she is meeting her lover, and you are imagining all of it.

So what does Theroux recommended we should read?

'*Madame Bovary* would be very high on my list,' he told me, '*Diary of a Nobody*, a Graham Greene novel, could be *The Heart of the Matter* or *Brighton Rock*, if you've never read *Huckleberry Finn* I would say that, if it was someone travelling in California I would say Patrick White, *A Fringe of Leaves*, a wonderful book, or *Riders in the Chariot*, if you're going to Alaska you should read *Riders in the Chariot*. You get the picture, none of those books would disappoint a reader.'

Cherry-Garrard's expeditioners had plenty of books on Arctic and Antarctic travel. But they were reference tools, useful for advice on how to line the tents or work a blubber stove.

I have experimented with both approaches.

Some years ago I walked with one of my daughters along the Thorsborne Trail, on the east side of Hinchinbrook Island in Queensland, around the Atherton tablelands and on to Cape Tribulation. She knew about maps, compasses, which rock to stand on in a fast-flowing stream, how to put up the tent, how to take it down, where to put your Swiss army knife so you could find it again, and how to sensibly pack food and all of life's comforts for enjoyable hiking.

She said we could take only two books, and I could choose. Why I packed Gitta Sereny's *Albert Speer: His Battle with Truth* I'm not exactly sure now—perhaps it was sufficiently big to last the entire length of the trip. I also took some short stories by Harold Brodkey and at Mulligan's Falls we sat on a rock and I read one aloud. It was about a mother who dies young and her son's efforts to re-create her from snippets of other people's conversations. We wept at the end—marvelling at the transcendent power of art to move us in this remote place.

Reading like this in a place very different from the subject matter of your book can be refreshing—especially if the beauty or the strangeness of the place is extreme, and reading allows you to rest your eyes and your body through exercising your imagination.

But I took exactly the opposite approach on a trip to Spain. In Granada, looking across to the Alhambra, the fourteenth-century palace and fortress built for the Muslim Nasrid dynasty and sunk into disrepair for centuries after their fall, I relished reading a book by nineteenth-century American writer Washington Irving. His *Tales of the Alhambra*, published in 1832, described his journey to Granada through rugged and dangerous country, with the risks of bandits at each bend in the road. He took enough money for his expenses, and a 'little surplus of hard dollars by way of *robber purse*, to satisfy the gentlemen of the road, should we be assailed. Unlucky is the too wary traveller who, having grudged this precaution, falls into their clutches empty handed: they are apt to give him a sound ribroasting for cheating them out of their dues.'

I was amused that the same warnings were current nearly two hundred years later, at the time of the Spanish debt and unemployment crisis. His descriptions of the inside of the palace were a pleasure to read with my own memories of the same rooms in mind.

Later, in Barcelona, I finally read George Orwell's *Homage to Catalonia*, and imagined the vicious battles in the streets of that city between the leftist groups that were supposed to be fighting fascism together.

In Southern France I read a history of the Cathars, whose fortress castles lie in ruins on peaks you can see from the charming villages below. Their long battles with the Catholic crusaders from the north, the tortures they suffered through the Inquisitions, their crazy theories that the world was created by the Devil, and their strictures against eating meat or milk, procreating and marriage, whirled around my mind. One night when the village celebrated 14 Juillet, I was woken by churchbells, loud techno music, mad dogs howling and local hoons fighting. For a moment I imagined the villagers as an angry thirteenth-century mob, torches aflame, out for blood.

I lived in Berlin for three months in 2001 to do some research and to learn German. I spent weekdays between 8.30 a.m. and 1.00 p.m. in the hothouse of my language class, with students from Japan, Korea, China, Uzbekistan and Croatia. Our fledgling German was the only *lingua franca*. Our teacher was brilliant, and in exemplary German fashion allowed no noodling around in the class. She choreographed every moment to gain the best possible result. It was truly marvellous and truly exhausting.

I spent my afternoons riding trains and getting the food shopping done. After I returned to the flat I was living in, ate and did my homework, it was an absolute relief to settle down with Alexandra Richie's *Faust's Metropolis:*

*A History of Berlin*, and swim in the rich past of the city I was living in.

'Like Faust,' she writes, 'Berlin can be said to have two spirits in the same breast; it is both a terrible and a wonderful city, and a place which has created and destroyed and whose name is both acclaimed and blackened.'

How different it is for the reader coming from Australia to comprehend the long history of a city like Berlin. How many hundreds of years it has taken for the place to get its shape, subject to the geographies of politics.

I lived on the old border between East and West Berlin, on the same street where the publishing magnate Axel Springer built a gleaming golden building in order to show the easterners looking over the wall the nature of western success, and so cause maximum irritation to the GDR authorities.

At the corner of Kommandant Strasse and Zimmerstrasse, there was a line of cobblestones in the street marking where the Berlin Wall used to run. Every morning, on my way to the U-Bahn station at Spittelmarkt, I hopped over the stones, imagining I was leaping between 1961 and 1989. Hitler's bunker was around the corner and the Museum of the Topography of Terror further along. I had passed it one day, but was on my way home to eat the delicious herring I had bought, so couldn't stop. I read Richie's book each day, and the next day walked the streets with an enlarged idea of the layers of meaning all around me.

A few weeks into my stay, I read in Richie about Klosterstrasse, now the U-Bahn station you emerged from if you were going to listen to some cool new music performer. But centuries ago, after the 1349 outbreak of plague, Berliners began to blame the Jews for poisoning the wells. Jews were violently attacked and moved for a time to a protected alley near the present Klosterstrasse, which was closed off at night by a huge iron gate. After this many fled to Poland. I was sure that these people helped to form the Jewish-Polish communities from which my parents came. Reading *Faust's Metropolis* in Berlin made the experience richer, deeper, ghostly and chilling.

Even a boat ride on the Spree—advertised as a literature tour of Berlin—was complicated. It had rained the whole day and I sat at the prow with an umbrella held low, listening to the tour guides perform Brecht readings and Kurt Weil songs. We passed by the bridge where the Polish-born German revolutionary Rosa Luxemburg was thrown in the Landwehr Canal. There was talk of naming it *Rosa Luxemburg Brücke* but naming a bridge after a communist seemed impossible in the post–Berlin Wall climate.

When I flew back to Australia I went to my *Faber Book of Reportage* again and found this entry from Rosa

Luxemburg's account of her term in Breslau Prison two years before she died:

> Here I am lying in a dark cell upon a mattress hard as stone; the building has its usual churchyard quiet, so that one might as well be already entombed; through the window there falls across the bed a glint of light from the lamp which burns all night in front of the prison. At intervals I can hear faintly in the distance the noise of a passing train or close at hand the dry cough of the prison guard as in his heavy boots, he takes a few slow strides to stretch his limbs. The gride of the gravel beneath his feet has so hopeless a sound that all the weariness and futility of existence seems to be radiated thereby into the damp and gloomy night. I lie here alone and in silence, enveloped in the manifold black wrappings of darkness, tedium, unfreedom and winter—and yet my heart beats with an immeasurable and incomprehensible inner joy, just as if I were moving in the brilliant sunshine across a flowery mead. And in the darkness I smile at life, as if I were the possessor of a charm which would enable me to transform all that is evil and tragical into serenity and happiness. But when I search my mind for the cause of this joy, I find there is no cause, and can only laugh at myself—I believe that the key to the riddle is simply life itself, this deep darkness of night is soft and beautiful as velvet, if only one looks at it in the right way. The gride of the damp

gravel beneath the slow and heavy tread of the prison guard is likewise a lovely little song of life—for one who has ears to hear.

I am so moved by this wisdom, by the spark of life that was hers to illuminate both her dark cell and our own lives, far removed in time and space. That's what is so precious in reading this way—you can plumb the depths of another's experience while sitting still with a book in your hands. Books that recount ordeals are precious because an ordeal is what we most fear, and the stories that tell us how to survive them reassure us about what a human being is capable of, as we survive our own lives every day, our own mysterious journeys.

## CHAPTER 14

# *A fine ash like snow*

———————

While we were still living in our flat across the road from St Kilda beach a set of old books came into our home. They had dark-brown calfskin covers and gold leaf on the edges of every page. A couple still had two clasps holding the covers together and were inlaid with mother-of-pearl.

They were Jewish Prayer books, for the different feasts of the year—Rosh Hashanah, Yom Kippur, Passover (this one is also called a 'Haggadah'), and the lesser known festivals of Shavuot and Sukkot. Our neighbour Lillian had been given them by her father. As her husband Tom (my comic-strip-reading companion) wasn't Jewish and she had ceased to practise her religion (her grown-up son George, although technically Jewish, had not had a bar mitzvah) she gave the books to my mother, who she said would have more use for them.

George was an actor and my mother took me to see him in Tennessee Williams' *The Night of the Iguana*, in which he took the starring role of Reverend Shannon, a failed cleric having a breakdown in Mexico. She took me backstage and I saw the dressing rooms where the men and women changed in front of each other. When I expressed surprise Mama said that the men weren't interested in the women anyway. I had no idea what she meant.

Now I can google George and see that he spent his early years in the Murray River town of Nangiloc, a sister town to Colignan (Nangiloc spelt backwards). These were both soldier-settlement towns that were established after World War One, but the land had been divided into blocks too small to be viable and most settlers had left by the 1930s. These five books must have spent time in Nangiloc before lying for twenty years on my mother's shelves, and for more than thirty on my own.

We read the Haggadah on the two nights of Passover. My father rushed through the prayers and the expositions so that we could start eating. Passover made my parents sad, as they remembered all their family Passovers with relatives who were later murdered.

I had a complex relationship with the five books from Lillian. They were old and musty. On facing pages was first the mysterious Hebrew text then an arcane English translation of equally mysterious goings-on in biblical times, and the commentaries of generations of rabbis since. I looked at the books and imagined them being printed long before the Holocaust, and staying together on the shelf in rural Australia and in St Kilda throughout the war, before arriving here on my parents' Passover table, silent and seemingly without the power to comfort those who dutifully recited their words or served the soup and matzo balls.

And now, another religious text stands next to these books on my shelf—this too a Haggadah covered in brown leather, but a facsimile of a medieval codex, printed in Yugoslavia in 1988. I bought it on a trip to the city of Sarajevo in 2001.

The story of how it came into my life is a strange and magical tale about a journey longer and more dramatic than that which took Lillian's five prayer books from Vienna, where they were first published, to London, where she was born, to Nangiloc and then to Melbourne.

There were very few relatives around when I grew up—and the Passover Seders were populated by my mother, my father, my sister and me. My mother had some third cousins in Australia, but a rift over something that was not explained to me had stopped them inviting us to their homes for Sunday afternoon teas. I had a crush on one of them. His name was Jaque, because he was born in transit in Paris and his Russian mother couldn't spell Jacques. He was two years my senior. Occasionally I saw him on campus at university; he was a man about town by then and ignored his younger cousin. Later I heard that he had joined the diplomatic service and then the UN and had a posting in Europe, so I contacted him during my time in Berlin.

We met for dinner, along with his boss, Ambassador Jacques Paul Klein, Special Representative of the Secretary-General of the UN mission in Bosnia and Herzegovina. After a long meal at which Jaque and Jacques Paul urged me to taste many kinds of vodka with bison grass, rye or other elements I can't fully remember, they told me about a medieval codex, the famed Sarajevo Haggadah, which had been created in Spain in the fourteenth century, then smuggled across Europe, hidden, rescued, hidden again, until, in 2001, just before the World Trade Center attacks, it was lying deep in a vault in a commercial bank in Sarajevo.

Late in the evening my hosts suggested that, if I could get myself to Sarajevo, they'd arrange a viewing of the manuscript for me. I was working as a journalist and thought it would make a great radio program. Who could resist?

I tried to find out as much as I could beforehand. It seemed that, in the early fourteenth century, a beautiful

Haggadah was created in Barcelona, possibly as a wedding present for two young people from important Sephardi Jewish families.

It was an unusual document. Despite an interpretation of the Old Testament warning against idolatry, this Haggadah began (reading from right to left) with thirty-four full-page miniatures, starting with the creation of the world and finishing with the death of Moses, and continued with an illuminated text and hymns and Torah readings. Until the Sarajevo Haggadah was discovered it was believed that there were no illustrations at all in Jewish texts.

It was transported from Spain, most probably in 1492 with the expulsion of the Jews during the Inquisition, and found its way to Italy. There the sale of the book is recorded in 1510. Another note on the book, dated 1609 by the Roman Censor Vistorini, declares that there is nothing objectionable in it from the standpoint of the Catholic Church.

The book made its way across the Adriatic Sea to Split, to Dubrovnik and finally to Sarajevo, possibly in the luggage of Jewish merchants in the eighteenth century.

In 1894 a young man from the Cohen family in Sarajevo brought the book to his school to sell it, as his family was destitute after his father's death. Versions of this story begin to have a touch of folklore about them.

The codex was then bought for a few dozen florins by the National Museum of Bosnia and Herzegovina and it was sent to Vienna for conservation. It was duly returned after two years. From then on it would be called the Sarajevo Haggadah, and was well known to scholars and collectors of rare manuscripts. Archivists say that it is the seminal Jewish codex of the Middle Ages. Well before the siege of Sarajevo it was a symbol of the city's survival and rejuvenation, as iconic as the bridge where Gavrilo Princip killed Archduke Ferdinand, thereby starting World War One, and the buildings that were erected for the 1984 Winter Olympics.

My journey on the trail of this medieval codex began with a flight from Berlin to Munich and on to Sarajevo. We tacked over the Alps and then down into valleys where scattered Bosnian mountain villages hugged the ridges. It was autumn but the hills around Sarajevo were mostly bare. During the siege of this town, just an hour away from Germany's richest city, which started in 1992, the trees had been cut down for firewood. As we prepared for landing we swept over large cemeteries that seemed too big for the place. The Muslim graves, clearly visible from the air, were marked with white mileposts rather than flat upright headstones. Chunks of the hills were simply blown away.

Jaque and his driver picked me up from the airport, and we drove into the city, past the bombarded large apartment blocks that had been built for the Olympics. Each window frame was charred, and sometimes the top of a building was sheared off. In some places you could see an attempt at renewal but the economy was still in the doldrums six years after the war had ended.

Here, and throughout Bosnia, libraries, archives, museums and cultural institutions had been targeted for destruction to remove any traces of evidence that people of different ethnic and religious groups had for generations lived and worked together.

On 25 August 1992 the century-old library of the National Museum of Bosnia and Herzegovina was shelled and burned. According to eyewitnesses braving the hail of sniper fire from Serbian nationalist positions across the river, librarians and other volunteers formed a human chain to pass books out of the burning building. Aida Buturovic, a librarian in the exchange section, was shot to death by a sniper while attempting to rescue books from the flames. Surviving staff members of the library—Serbs, Croats, Muslims and Jews—continued with the rescue and ten per cent of its collection was saved.

Three months earlier, Sarajevo's Oriental Institute—home to the largest collection of Islamic and Jewish manuscripts and Ottoman documents in south-eastern Europe—was shelled with phosphorous grenades and burned. A total of 5263 bound manuscripts in Arabic,

Persian, Hebrew and Aljamiado (a Bosnian Slavic language written in Arabic script) were destroyed, along with 7000 Ottoman documents, primary source material for five centuries of Bosnian history, a collection of nineteenth-century cathedral registers and 200,000 other documents of the Ottoman era.

In each case the library and the Oriental Institute alone were targeted, leaving buildings on either side standing. Eyewitnesses described a fine ash like snow falling over the city.

The Sarajevo Haggadah escaped this bombardment. It was rescued by a Muslim, Dr Enver Imamović, the director of the museum. It had reportedly been stored in an old Viennese safe, which saved it from incineration.

By the time I got to the city in 2001, the building where the Sarajevo Haggadah was housed before the 1992 war was still a ruin. The windows were covered with planks of wood. On another site, the philosophy department of Sarajevo University had been heavily shelled. A tall building next door to the university stood silent—every window discharged, every room bared to its concrete roots by searing fires.

This was on the main boulevard, formerly known as Ulica Zmaja od Bosne or 'Dragon of Bosnia Street', which had earned a new name: Sniper's Alley. Further down the street, walking through the historic part of Sarajevo, it was much like many other old East European towns, mostly rundown low-rise buildings. The minarets on the mosques were the highest structures. Side by side or around the corner were synagogues and churches, both Catholic and Orthodox. A tap with free-flowing spring water, from the hills that surround the city, runs at the centre of the old market, and I drank from it with my cupped hands. Modern Muslim women passed, with beautiful faces and elegant headscarves and kohl around their eyes.

Out-of-work men, some playing backgammon, hung around the main square and the little streets leading off it. I saw people with vacant eyes, madmen obsessively crossing themselves, and one fellow rushing through the market clutching his hand to his heart. I wondered what he had seen or done. Men missing limbs were pushed by their families in broken wheelchairs.

The roofs in the streets of jewellery makers and samovar sellers and carpet weavers were crumbling. I walked down narrow alleyways with hardly enough room for two people to pass. These opened into yet another square where tables and chairs filled every available space and were packed with people drinking coffee under umbrellas, talking, talking, talking. Sarajevo may have been traumatised by war but it was pulsing with life.

There were rarely any road signs to tell you where to park or how to navigate. The house-numbering system was eccentric, subject to the vicissitudes of previous bouts of shelling and target practice. In the evenings you could hear the muezzin calling people to prayer from the raised minarets, with the aid of a tinny loudspeaker.

I met Dr Jakob Finci, president of Sarajevo's 700-person strong Jewish community, and the head of La Benevolencija, the community's educational, cultural and philanthropic organisation. He is now Bosnia's ambassador to Switzerland. He told me the history of Jews in Bosnia dated to 1530 when the first Jewish family settled there. Bosnia was a province of the Ottoman Empire, which treated Jews like all other non-Muslims of the time—no ghetto and no special persecution save for the prohibition against Jews owning land.

Life was relatively good for Jews in Sarajevo until the Nazi invasion in 1941, when the pro-fascist Croatian government facilitated the removal and murder of Jews in local slaughters and in more remote concentration camps. Finci's own parents were sent to the Italian camp in which he was born at the end of the war. He is the only Finci in the last three hundred and fifty years not to have been born in Sarajevo. Eighty per cent of the community's twelve thousand members were murdered.

In 1941 German soldiers and local gangs destroyed the Old Jewish Temple, the sacred objects in it, and a large library collection including the archive of the Sarajevo Jewish community.

Finci is passionate about the Haggadah story. 'I think that the story that the Haggadah was hidden in the library was a realistic one,' he told me. 'But it's not romantic enough and being a romantic I would like to think it was hidden somewhere in the mountains near Sarajevo and that it was saved yet again.'

Kemal Bakarsic was, from 1986 to 1993, chief librarian of the National Museum of Bosnia and Herzegovina. He was also custodian of the Sarajevo Haggadah. Once a year he would check the condition of the codex, which was kept in a vault at the library, but never exhibited. Facsimile versions, like mine, were available to scholars and others.

By the time I was there, he was teaching bibliography at the University of Sarajevo and I went to visit him. I climbed several flights of stairs through clouds of thick cigarette smoke. It seemed that every young person smoked, and I could see the need for calming of nerves. Why think of emphysema and cancer when so recently there was no thought of a future at all?

Bakarsic's office was full of paper and books and the results of his hobby of making jigsaw puzzles from Escher prints, an enterprise that seemed tailor-made to drive one to madness. He told me he was still obsessed with the Haggadah. He described the people who are attracted to it as seekers, retrievers and keepers. He's a keeper. Seekers are always inventing ideas and trying to find out what has happened. They are gossips and narrators searching for the story. Retrievers are convinced that the seekers have failed in their quest.

This particular codex has dozens of stories surrounding it: several about how it came to Bosnia, three about how it was sold to the national museum, five versions about what happened to it during World War Two and ten new stories for the period between 1992 and 1995.

The margin note in the codex dated 1609 showing that the book was passed by the customs office in Rome is the only thing known about it until it was sold in 1894 for 150 golden crowns to the museum. This gap of almost three centuries is filled with stories.

Bakarsic said that the first story, which he calls a legend, is about a young Jew from Bosnia, a student in Padua, who fell in love with a beautiful girl and received the Haggadah codex as his wedding present.

The second legend is of a Jewish merchant from Sarajevo who had saved his Italian companion from a bad business deal in Florence and received the Haggadah as reward.

The private nature of the Passover feasts at which Haggadahs are used adds to the difficulty of knowing exactly how this Haggadah arrived in Sarajevo, and what happened to it before the museum bought it at the end of the nineteenth century.

Bakarsic told me that the rumours about the codex in World War Two have their roots in Bosnian folk tradition. The basic story is that in 1941, shortly after occupation, a German officer came to the museum and demanded from the director the extradition of the Haggadah. The director explained that another officer had asked for and received the codex just half an hour earlier. The director then smuggled the manuscript to a village in the hills surrounding the city, where it was hidden under a pear tree—or in other versions, an apple tree or even a cherry tree—or under the floorboards of a mosque in the care of a Muslim cleric. After the liberation of the city the Haggadah was returned to the museum.

In Bosnia, Bakarsic told me, on the birth of a son, the father buries a barrel of his best wine or brandy under a tree. When the young man's wedding day arrives, the barrel is dug up and the liquor drunk at the celebrations.

After the war the director of the museum and the chief librarian were accused by the communists of being collaborators with the Nazis. Perhaps the story about the rescue of the Haggadah, Bakarsic said, was that they did not resist the Germans, but they did rescue this Jewish text and risked their lives doing so.

In the most recent conflict, the Haggadah was once again the subject of gossip: it had been sold to buy arms for the Bosnian Muslim government. It had been damaged beyond repair. It was found in bushes after the Serb shelling of the museum. It was rescued from rising waters from the museum's basement.

None of the above was true. In fact the codex was taken from the museum vault and put into the National Bank vault for safe-keeping. Bakarsic himself was elevated to the position of deputy minister of Science, Culture, Education and Sport in the Bosnian government between 1993 and the 1995 Dayton Accords. He took the rumours of mistreatment of the Haggadah rather personally. He describes the 1995 Passover celebration Seder by the Jewish community as a 'humiliation' for the Bosnian government. President Izebekovic was pressured into showing the intact Haggadah at the event, to scotch the rumours that it had been traded for arms.

Some weeks after our dinner in Berlin, I met Ambassador Jacques Paul Klein again in his office at the UN compound, a previously burned-out student residence at the university. The codex was of interest to him in his role coordinating UNESCO and UNICEF cultural matters on items that need to be preserved for international common interests.

When he arrived in Sarajevo he discovered that the Haggadah was housed in a bank vault, probably deteriorating, and in need of further restoration. There was no money and people were quarrelling over the manuscript. It was difficult for him even to see it. The story of the life of this book was taking absurd turns.

Klein was a big man with a booming voice and large hands that moved the air in front of him as he explained his vision for the Sarajevo Haggadah. A facsimile was open on the desk in front of him, and he thumbed through it to show me his favourite pages. He wondered at the illustrations showing the human form, which seemed to violate Talmudic law. Had its makers been influenced by Flemish and French prayer books and bibles of the same period?

Klein wanted the museum to build a special air-conditioned room for the codex. Bakarsic wasn't sure. He was concerned about the fragile collection of butterflies and other insects, the herbarium and the lack of heating in the building. He wanted to see the museum reconstructed as a small version of the Smithsonian—full of people and 'fancy exhibits', and with money for the future development of the collections. 'Including of course the protection of the Haggadah, which is the jewel in the crown.'

In the meantime, Bakarsic was trying to re-create electronic replicas of many of the rare manuscripts that had been burnt. Some of them existed in photocopied form in other countries. He talked of a 'suicidal mission' to try to locate every scholar who ever went to the Oriental Institute in Sarajevo and made a copy or a transcript of any of the former manuscripts. He showed me a bad photocopy of an Arabic text that was in his desk drawer—in fact it has become the new original now that this manuscript has gone up in the smoke of Sarajevo.

On my last day in Sarajevo I was due to see the famous codex. It was a misty autumn morning. By 11 a.m. the fog had hardly lifted over the surrounding hills, but it was going to be warm. I met Jakob Finci in the forecourt of the Union Bank. The manuscript was kept safe in its treasury.

Finci seemed excited to be seeing the Haggadah again. We waited for the representatives of the Sarajevo Museum, the bank, and a couple of visiting curators from New York and Jerusalem, and were then escorted down the stairs, through a big blue security checkpoint, and then to the gleaming vault where locked boxes surrounded a round white table and a suite of blue office chairs. The key was found, and a box in the upper corner of the vault was opened. Inside it was a royal blue metal box, with the wax seals of the museum and the paper seals of the bank intact.

They were broken by the security guards and the box was opened to reveal layers of white tissue paper. These were parted and an official wearing white cotton gloves lifted the book out of the box. It was about the size of a paperback novel. Its 1894 binding was worn and split but this was the only part of the Haggadah in any need of repair. It sat on the tissue paper and invited opening. The plates were surprisingly bright, glowing. The first is a picture of the creation of the world, the light and the dark. I was surprised to see the world depicted as a globe. The last plate depicts the death of Moses.

Gold and copper illuminations, thirty-four full-page miniatures, blues, reds, greens, nearly seven hundred years old, radiated from the beautiful pages. And then the evidence of the book's domestic life: wine stains, a father's notes, children's scribbles, on one page clearly a young child's penmanship of the Hebrew letter Gimmel.

The ink had been applied with a wide-nibbed implement, so that some letters showed a full-nibbed stroke at the top of the letter leading to thinner strokes at the bottom. There was a concentrated beauty in the illustrations and the square Hebrew letters. There was humour in the cheeky bird-like figures. How many lifetimes had it seen, how many close escapes from immolation?

My visit was over in half an hour. I drove past the university, the UN compound, the torched high-rise flats to the airport. I waited with a group of English town-planners who had been at a conference in the shell of the city. The plane was late and they were going to miss their London connection. Eyebrows were raised.

When I made my radio documentary about my visit, my last words were:

As we took off from Sarajevo airport I thought of the city cut off from the world by the siege, of a nation

divided by nationalistic passions, which overflowed
with cruelty and blood, of the libraries on fire, of books
being used as fuel for heating and cooking, of people
digging under pear and apple trees to find barrels of
brandy or wine and of a priceless medieval codex with
vibrant illustrations of strange and cheeky animals. And
how the small mysterious book might build mutual
understanding again, and bring people together, as they
used to live for centuries.

A naive hope? Of course. The peace agreement that was
finally brokered divides the country into three communities—Bosnian Muslims, Croats and Serbs. Only institutions that speak to each group's national identity receive
any financial support from government. Multiculturalism
is almost dead. It's reported that all of Bosnia's cultural
institutions are on the brink of termination. The staff of
the museum haven't been paid for months. There is no
money for climate control and little for lighting.

Kemal Bakarsic died of cancer in 2006. Both my
cousin Jaque and Ambassador Klein have left the UN.
Jakob Finci, who was elected to chair a national committee
charged with setting up a truth-and-reconciliation com-
mission and who was appointed head of the civil service
agency, took the Bosnian government to court in Strasbourg
for a breach of the European convention on human rights.
The court ruled at the end of 2011 that no exclusion based

'on a person's ethnic origin is capable of being objectively justified in a contemporary democratic society'. But the result of the Dayton Accords, which brought an end to the war in 1995, was that membership in the upper house of parliament is reserved for equal numbers of Bosnian Muslims, Croats and Serbs. Other groups, including Jews and the Roma, are effectively excluded. As Jakob Finci is not a member of any of the three communities, he is barred from public office in his country.

Since my visit, a special vault has been built in the restored National Museum, equipped with bullet-proof glass to protect the Haggadah, which is now insured for more than a billion dollars. This small medieval codex, witness to seven hundred years of history and dispute, sits there now, awaiting the next part of its story.

## CHAPTER 15

# Genius from the dust

On the shelf behind me as I write are two sets of children's books—an eight-volume set of a 1930 edition of *Cassell's Book of Knowledge* and a ten-volume 1947 edition of Arthur Mee's *The Children's Encyclopaedia*, first published in 1909.

I haven't read through them. Sometimes, books arrive in such a way as to be forever tainted with the stories they bring.

In my late twenties I got married again, for a short time, to another man whose knowledge and intellectual abilities impressed me. His talents included mathematics, translation from Italian (not his first language), a forensic memory of French films of the 1960s and a sweeping familiarity with political history.

At some stage he brought these children's encylopaedias into my life. They had been important to him when he was growing up and acquiring his impressive range of interests. He liked multi-volume sets so much that on the first of his birthdays we spent together he asked for a volume of the *Collected Works of Marx and Engels*. His ambition was to own the entire fifty-volume set of everything ever written by his political heroes.

The place to buy them was the International Book Shop, which you got to through a nondescript doorway and then up some stairs in Elizabeth Street in the middle of Melbourne. Here every kind of left-wing publication could be found.

For each of my presents to him I climbed these stairs. The International Book Shop never seemed to have the whole set at any one time, so I started with Volume 3. I thought we'd be together forever, and didn't try to get Volume 1 or 2 before I branched out to Volume 10. I had endless time to buy the complete set.

My second ex-husband told me that when he was a university student he found a job as an orderly in a large psychiatric hospital. He got to know one particular patient, an old man, who said he wasn't mad at all, but a gifted genius who had been writing a massive project, which he called 'The Snowball Book of Knowledge'. It was a most important work.

The old man was distressed that his manuscript was still in his shack, somewhere in a forest near a remote country town. He told the student orderly its exact whereabouts, and, one weekend, the young man took off on his Vespa scooter armed with a hand-drawn map.

Now, as I write, I can see the mythic elements assembling themselves—a mad old man (an ancient mariner?), a secret book of knowledge, a young man on a quest—and I am shaking my head as I remember the rest of the story. The student arrives at a rundown shack, he parks the Vespa, his heart beats faster and he climbs in through a broken window.

He finds the room in which The Snowball Book of Knowledge is kept and discovers pages strewn around the floor, some of them wet with the rain that is blowing in through the broken window. Some pages have been nibbled by rats and other hungry creatures. I remember being so sad for the old man on hearing this, and so impressed with my ex-husband who went to rescue the book and the man's reputation.

But when he read the old man's pages he was terribly disappointed. The Snowball Book of Knowledge was simply a notebook in which the old man recorded all the things that he had ever heard about. Things that everyone who had been to school already knew. Five plus five is ten. The capital of Australia is Canberra.

I seem to remember that he didn't take the pages back to the old gent because he didn't want him to see how messed up his pages were. His life's work. Maybe he told him he couldn't find the hut.

What strikes me now is the disappointment of the young man. He really thought that he might have discovered a secret key to the meaning of life. I thought it was a romantic story with a wistful ending, but I could have saved myself a lot of wasted time and indeed some money if I had questioned my grip on reality.

As it is, I only bought five volumes of the *Collected Works of Marx and Engels*. We parted long before he could amass the whole set. I imagine that his subsequent paramours have contributed in their own ways to the collection.

And I am left with Arthur Mee's and Cassell's sets of books, which he didn't take with him—a silent reminder to be a little more discerning in my choice of men. In some ways they now add up to my own Snowball Book of Knowledge.

Alongside the children's encyclopaedias on my shelves are several sets of books that I have only ever dipped into. These are my beautiful boxed sets of mysterious classics, and I have a fantasy that, if I live to be a very old woman, I will properly learn all the languages that fascinate me and I will read my boxed sets of the world's classic literature.

Here is *The Tale of Genji*. It was written in eleventh-century Japan, almost exactly a thousand years ago, by a lady-in-waiting at the imperial court, a woman known to posterity as Murasaki Shikibu. Readers began to acknowledge the tale as a classic within a century of its writing, and it soon became an object of intense study. The story starts when a woman of lower rank in the court gives birth to a son called Genji. He is favoured by the emperor because he's so beautiful, talented and likeable. He goes on to have many affairs, which allows Murasaki Shikibu to explore ideas of love, court politics, friendship, life and death—all the things that make a wonderful story.

In 2008 I interviewed Royall Tyler, a scholar of Japanese language and literature, a translator and, incidentally, an alpaca farmer in New South Wales. His translation of *The Tale of Genji*, all 1184 pages and 54 chapters, including 795 poems, took him almost ten years. How many years has it taken me not to read it, and how long will it take me when I do read it? The plot summary above is what Royall Tyler told me it was about, not something that I have discovered myself. Yet.

I was speaking to him about his approach to translation so it was not important for me to read the whole work. But by the following summer I had time to read more of *The Tale of Genji*. I found that the earlier stories about concubines, stepmothers and secrets gave way to more complex and less interesting tales of court life. I was confused about the characters. Apart from Genji no one is called by their personal names. If they have no official title they are called, for example, the Lady of the House. If they change jobs, they change titles. Even if the naming is true to the social hierarchies of eleventh-century Japan the book demented me. I was defeated.

I look at the boxed set and admire the illustration on the cover of Genji as a grown man wearing wide trousers and a kimono lined in red. I like the red linen-bound volumes and the line drawings in the text. I think of Murasaki Shikibu, who was born in about 973. She was the daughter of a provincial governor of Japan, a middle level of the aristocracy which, in the capital Kyoto, supplied ladies-in-waiting to the greatest lords and ladies around the emperor. She was called to serve as a lady-in-waiting to the Empress Shôshi. Nobody knows just when she began her story, or indeed when it was finished. People speculate that she died in 1013 but, again, the truth isn't known.

And it wasn't unusual by her time for a woman to write. The official written language at the court in Kyoto was Middle Chinese, even though the courtiers did not speak it. These men studied history, philosophy and religious texts and wrote poetry in Chinese. But the women wrote in Japanese, as different from modern Japanese as the English of *Beowulf* is from the language we speak. I wonder what happened to Murasaki. The book finishes in the middle of a sentence, and scholars speculate on whether she intended this, or left her story incomplete.

Next to *The Tale of Genji* sits a boxed volume of *The Icelandic Sagas*, abridged and introduced by Magnus Magnusson, with beautifully strange illustrations by Simon Noyes. I fell upon this when I decided that self-improvement was in order once I started working on my first literary program, *Books and Writing*. *The Icelandic Sagas* are stories of the Norwegian Viking settlers who made their home in Iceland, of their land disputes and marriages and many deaths by axe. My friend and brilliant essayist Eliot Weinberger describes it as:

> An enormous 'human comedy' of love, greed, rage, lust, marriages and property settlements, travels, revenge, funerals and festivals, meetings, abductions, prophetic dreams and strange coincidences, fish and sheep. Nearly everyone in Iceland is descended from these people, and they know the stories, and the stories of what happened in the generations since.

One of my favourite of Weinberger's essays is simply a list of dreams found in the sagas that begins:

> Þorbjörg of Indriðastaðir dreamed that eighty wolves passed by with flames coming from their mouths, and among them was a white bear.

> Glaumvör dreamed that a bloody sword was sticking

out from her husband's tunic, and that a river ran
through the house, sweeping away all their things.

Hersteinn Blund-Ketillson dreamed he saw his father
on fire.

It was wonderful to imagine that these might have been
the real dreams of people a thousand years ago, which had
made their way into these histories/sagas/stories, and I was
hearing about them as if I were at breakfast with the characters the morning after.

The same summer I tackled *Genji*, I took my abridged
*Icelandic Sagas* from my shelf. But, oh, how many pages
you had to get through to reach each dream. Too many
for me, and I was thankful for Eliot Weinberger who had
done the spadework. You had to read through an awful lot
of genealogical records—who was married to whom and
whose daughters and sons they were—before you got to
the stories. And some of the stories did seem to be about
legal disputes, multigenerational feuds and the way they
were solved. Many of them ended with an axe-hammer
blow to the head. The charming Icelandic naming pattern which, to this day, insists on the use of traditional first
names combined with the last name—using the mother or
father's first name plus 'son' or 'dottir'— mean that many
of the characters in the Sagas have the same name or one
pretty similar. In Egil's Saga there are characters called

Thorvald, Thorunn, two Thorsteins, two Thorulfs, three Thorgeirs, and four Thoros. I have no patience.

My three-volume set of the *Arabian Nights* stands next to my Vikings. I read an abridged version as a child. I can still feel the tension in the story of Scheherazade, the woman who told tales to save her own life. The *Arabian Nights* first appeared in Europe, translated into French by Antoine Galland, in twelve volumes between 1704 and 1717, and it was translated into English in 1708. It was woven out of tales told by the new bride Scheherazade to prevent her husband Shahryar the king from murdering her. He had been slaying virgins at a rate of knots ever since being cuckolded by a previous wife.

On the night of their marriage, Scheherazade begins to tell the king a tale, but she stops before it ends, forcing her husband to let her live another day so that she can continue. But the next night, although she completes the first story, she starts a new one, and leaves off so that she gets a second reprieve. This goes on for a thousand and one nights.

I knew that the *Arabian Nights* was an important book for my self-improvement plan. It had been astonishingly influential, and has inspired music, other stories, films and operas, as well as changing tastes in fashion and furniture—all that orientalism brought to the west. It had an enormous influence on the history of English literature,

French literature and that of many other European countries, and ultimately it came back to have influence on Arabian literature via its influence on the magical realism of Latin-American writers who were then translated into Arabic.

Some of the best-known stories, including those of Aladdin, Ali Baba and Sinbad, were not even part of the original manuscript. In his translation, Galland worked from a fourteenth-century Syrian text, and he added tales he'd collected in his own travels, including one he wrote down after a conversation with a Maronite Syrian who gave him the story of Aladdin. And he also changed the manuscript so that it had a stronger narrative line, omitting many of the poetic sections and adding details that accorded with eighteenth-century French taste.

In 1885 an English version was published by my old friend the British explorer and orientalist and translator of the *Kama Sutra*, Sir Richard Burton, in an erotic, private edition for subscribers.

Even as I open the books now, and read from the first 'framing' story, the pattern—of a story that is cut off when dawn breaks, so that the storyteller lives another day, and takes up the thread the next night—quickly begins to wear thin. Sometimes the stories are so 'nested', a story within a story within a story, that I close the book.

I also admit defeat with *The Mabinogion* (medieval

Celtic tales), *The Mahabharata* (the Hindu classic), *The Iliad* and parts of *The Odyssey*. I am struck by the popularity of stories that become other stories and shape-changing, as in Ovid's *Metamorphoses*, and would be interested to read an essay on why we like them so much, rather than wade through the stories themselves.

I remember essayist and novelist Geoff Dyer's words:

> The strange thing about this is that at twenty I imagined I would spend my middle age reading books that I didn't have the patience to read when I was young. But now, at forty-one, I don't even have the patience to read the books I read when I was twenty.

My impulse to read the great works of literature comes from my romantic yearning to understand the wisdom of the ages. I wonder what I might have read if Ptolemy's Royal Library of Alexandria had not been destroyed. I daydream about its papyrus scrolls which contained that world's complete collection of knowledge.

I am not alone. The search for scraps of papyrus grew into a quest in Napoleon's time for the great lost works of Greek literature. The first papyrus text ever to be published from findings at Faiyum in Egypt turned out to be a rather boring account of people who were digging out the irrigation ditches at the oasis there.

Then excavations at Pompeii and Herculaneum in the

mid-eighteenth century fired up the romantic imagination all over again. Scrolls from the Villa of the Papyri in Herculaneum were identified, after they had been mistaken for lumps of charcoal by excavation workers, who used them to light the torches at the dig. That stopped when the lumps were found to contain traces of writing. But what did they say?

Wordsworth wanted to know. This is how he ends his poem 'September 1819':

> O ye, who patiently explore
> The wreck of Herculanean lore,
> What rapture! could ye seize
> Some Theban fragment, or unroll
> One precious, tender-hearted scroll
> Of pure Simonides.
>
> That were, indeed, a genuine birth
> Of poesy; a bursting forth
> Of genius from the dust:
> What Horace gloried to behold,
> What Maro loved, shall we enfold?
> Can haughty Time be just!

This wishful thinking chimes with images of the people of Herculaneum gathering their most precious books together in an attempt to flee to safety as Vesuvius erupts, and the ash and mud comes raining down on them.

The papyrologists, on the other hand, were faced with crumbling blackened rolls. These carbonised papyri are like a rolled-up newspapers after a fire. You can still identify the rolls, and painstakingly peel off the fragments and, if you're lucky, the ancient Greek script might be present in maddening tiny pieces.

Till now, the only surviving fragments tell of a collection of Epicurian philosophical writings, mostly by Philodemus of Gadara, whose sentences are said to be rather tedious. Romantic bubble-bursters have even suggested the villa was being remodelled by a new owner at the time of the eruption, and the unremarkable papyri were all tossed in together in the renovation chaos.

But possibilities for romance still linger. Digital imaging spectroscopy has already helped read the black ink on the blackened papyrus of the scrolls, and hopes are that applications of CT scanning might even allow us to read the others without the need for damaging them further by unrolling them.

The idea of what a book might say can be even more powerful than its actual words. Two books sit, one upon the other, on a stand in the corner of my room. They are old books, hardbacks, but, like the papyri of Herculaneum, I don't know what's inside them. An artist friend gave them to me when she and her husband came for lunch one day. The books were from her recent exhibition about bees and temples. She had put them in a beehive and they had become encased by wax. She was interested in death, poetry and metamorphosis, and was full of wonder at how the bees had transformed these books.

She had been having a series of bad headaches. She had just turned sixty, and was beautiful and a little delicate. That day she explained that as a child she had survived leukaemia. She had been given radiotherapy and was told that she probably wouldn't ever be able to have children. In her thirties she had surprised everyone, including herself, by giving birth to twins. But she was haunted by her near misses, by the gifts of life, by the numinous world and by mortality.

I did not know her well but when I heard that she loved German literature I lent her my copies of Joseph Roth's *What I Saw: Reports from Berlin, 1920–1933*, and *My Prizes: An Accounting* by Thomas Bernhard, which was a hysterical collection recounting the bad grace with which the ornery Austrian writer had received various accolades. I remember that day my friend was wearing a beautifully cut long dark coat that suited her well. I thought she would enjoy the books as I placed her gift of beeswaxed volumes on the stand.

A few weeks later we heard that she had been diagnosed with a brain tumour, and after some months she died. At her funeral service her coffin stood on a bier surrounded by beeswax candles that had been part of her exhibition.

The waxed books are here as I write. I wonder what they are about but I don't want to disturb the wax that encloses them. They might be a message from the grave. They might not be. If they turned out to be geometry texts or military histories or manuals on irrigation ditches, might they lose the quality that makes them mysterious when I see them on the stand, reminding me of my friend, that lunch, her coat and the fleeting nature of life?

CHAPTER 16

# A good disposition

---

They wear ragged clothes and two of them have no shoes, but the three young boys in the photograph are hunched over a book that is sitting on the lap of the middle boy, his knees showing through his trousers. It is 1915, World War One is raging and in the city of Esztergom, the old capital of Hungary, not far from Budapest, the boys in their grubby caps forget their cold limbs and are transported by the book, but to where?

The photographer was André Kertész, born at the end of the nineteenth century. He liked to photograph readers of all descriptions, and all his life he did so from Hungary to Paris to New York. He published a book of these pictures, called *On Reading*.

In another Kertész photograph, taken in 1944, another

boy is caught in an act of pure pleasure. In the doorway of a New York shop under a sign saying *Paper is needed now! Bring it at any time*, he eats an ice cream on a messy pile of newspapers spilling onto the street, his focus on a page of comic strips.

On balconies, and rooftops, among chimney pots and washing lines, people snatch reading time, utterly engrossed and devoted only to their books.

In 1948 by the Medici Fountain in Paris, a couple read on folding wooden chairs, their faces turned from us towards the words in the book. Is it poetry? Are they illicit lovers? I imagine my mama reading there with a man she has met in the gardens, while my father plays cards in a café, oblivious to what my mother is doing in another part of the forest. Banned books were not the only forbidden fruit my mother enjoyed. But that is a story for another time.

And on an ancient edition of Voltaire, in New York in 1969, a beetle is snapped by Kertész, lost in contemplation of the paper beneath its feet, a last meal, perhaps, for a Kafka character?

*On Reading* was first published in 1971 and an exhibition followed in the UK and USA in 2009. The pictures in this book remind us of the private and reverential pleasure of reading, how it transports us from our prosaic lives to anywhere we care to imagine. While our world looks small on the outside, it's huge on the inside, in the magical spaces between the page and our absorption.

When I was growing up, I knew children whose parents would exclaim that they were 'doing nothing' if they were found with a book in their hands. They had to help around the house or go outside and do some real playing. The book was at best a distraction from what they ought to be doing, at worst a corrupter of young minds or a sissy enterprise.

But in none of the Kertész images does anyone read a book with a pencil or pen in their hand. Until recently I never read a book without taking notes. I already had something to write on—the book itself was my work desk.

My mother taught me to revere books. I once saw her kissing one of the books in a prayer-book set that I had accidently dropped. I had never before seen her do this, but she explained it was an old habit from her ultra-orthodox childhood where, she said, there was a rule and a prayer for everything, including dropping the sacred words.

But just before the turn of the century, when I began to read books for money as well as for love, I employed all formerly forbidden practices to get close to the book. And if that meant dog-earing the pages, writing questions in the end notes, and underlining and marking the text itself, so be it. Because things are different when the point of reading is not simply pleasure of self-improvement or wiling the days away, but working towards having a conversation with the author. For this you need to be prepared.

So I would read with several tracks in my head. One track is the way anybody reads for enjoyment: getting lost in the words and the story and the characters. The other tracks have questions attached: how does the writer know about this or that setting or historical moment or the work practices of horse whisperers or whale hunters or philosophers? Why does this character feel, say, do that? This book made me think such-and-such—was that what the writer wanted? How did the writer make me care? How did they paint a picture in my mind with mere word-strokes?

Apart from forming questions, I took note of sentences, phrases, words. I tried to isolate a few paragraphs or pages that the author might read to give people a flavour of the tone or the voice of the book. Sometimes it was better not to let the speaking voice of the author spoil the beautiful prose. My notes transcribed my conversation with the book.

If I'm sounding like an engineer rather than a reader, that was my task: to engineer a conversation. And like any journey over a beautiful bridge, I wanted to admire the span and be sure I would survive the crossing. I hoped that the engineer had done the calculations properly and that the bridge would remain standing. I needed to think about how the conversation might begin, where it might go, and what sights to point out along the way. This makes for very particular reading.

This kind of reading could make it hard to relax with a book on holidays. Each time I took out a book to read, I would find myself reading with a view to talking about it. I would reach for a writing implement. To cure myself of this habit I tried to read only dead authors on holiday. How could I interview them? But my mind would wander to ideas of interviewing their biographers, for example, and the pen would come out. Just one book, I'd say to myself, just one interview prepared before I go back to work. And then one became two, two became four and by mid-holiday I was once more working flat out.

As an interim measure I decided to study French again, and used my summers to sit with a private teacher at my kitchen table several times a week. The idea was for me to start reading only French novels on holidays. I was almost sure I wouldn't find myself interviewing these authors, as I was broadcasting only in English.

It never occurred to me to cure myself by vowing not to read at all. That would be like vowing not to breathe.

Finally I decided to find a mid-path. I would read for self-improvement, which was a kind of work, but I would read only dead people whose biographies had been long discussed and shelved.

I began to seek out the Penguin Classics series, the

black spines with a purple stripe across the top. I started with Suetonius's *The Twelve Caesars*. I felt as though I was entering a foreign country without a map.

But to my complete surprise the translation by Robert Graves introduced me to a world of intrigue, gossip and reportage that was like a contemporary report from the capital—be it London, Washington or Canberra. Suetonius told me all about Julius Caesar's rise to political power, his marriages, his love affairs and his errors. I learned that he was embarrassed about being bald, and combed his hair forwards, and that he was rumoured to remove hair from other parts of his body. He was said to have had an affair with King Nicomedes IV of Bithynia in Anatolia, and was called the 'Queen of Bithynia' in some quarters. He was also a great womaniser and among his mistresses was Cleopatra. In fact he had a law drawn up to legitimise his marriage to any woman he wanted 'for the procreation of children'. He was not a drinker. His enemy Marcus Cato said he was 'the only sober man who ever tried to wreck the Constitution'.

I like the fact that I smile at Cato's joke, that the defender of the Roman Republic who died in 46 BC can give me pleasure so far from his world and his time. Two millennia later, Suetonius can horrify me with reports of Caligula's madness and cruelty, his troubling mental illness, his 'over-confidence and extreme timorousness' as a despiser of gods, who was afraid of thunder.

Suetonius can whisper like a fashion blogger, telling us that Caligula wore an embroidered and precious-stone-encrusted cloak at public appearances teamed with silk forbidden to men and women's dresses over military boots or women's shoes:

> Often he affected a golden beard and carried a thunder bolt, trident, or serpent-twined staff in his hand.
> He even dressed up as Venus and, even before his expedition, wore the uniform of a triumphant general, including sometimes the breastplate which he had stolen from Alexander the Great's tomb at Alexandria.

Suetonius remarks that 'such frantic and reckless behaviour roused murderous thoughts in certain minds'. When Caligula died at twenty-nine after ruling for just over three years, I was relieved.

I was on the edge of my seat at the historian's description of the Emperor Claudius, whose own mother called him 'a monster: a man whom Nature had not finished but had merely begun'. When Claudius hid behind a curtain on hearing of the murder of his nephew Caligula, fearing for his own life, he was found by a soldier who, in a scene from a French farce, saw his feet sticking out. And instead of being killed he was proclaimed emperor. He died fourteen years later, a dish of mushrooms and a gruel chaser deliberately poisoned.

Suetonius was a friend and employee of the writer and magistrate Pliny the Younger, whose book *The Letters of the Younger Pliny* I turned to next. There's an added intimacy in reading these letters from the wealthy landowner, lawyer, writer and poet to his friends, to his beloved wife, to the historian Tacitus, to the emperor Trajan and to those who ask favours and advice.

Pliny is proud of the life he lives at his country estate. He describes his villa and its gardens and invites people to come and stay and talk with him. I want to visit too.

He gives a detailed account to Tacitus of the death of his uncle, Pliny the Elder, the writer and philosopher who tried to rescue his friends by ship after Vesuvius had erupted, destroying Pompeii and Herculaneum in 79 AD. Pliny the Younger was eighteen years old and staying with his uncle in Misenum, across the Bay of Naples from the volcano. It's a dramatic eyewitness description of the cloud on the horizon, the broad sheets of fire and leaping flames, the falling ash and stones and the smell of sulphur in the darkness at noon.

The elder Pliny tried to cross the bay against advice, and was defeated by the fierceness of the elements. His body was found two days later.

I admire Pliny the Elder, so I find his *Natural History* and discover the ancient world's encyclopaedic book of agriculture, astronomy, geography, metallurgy, architecture, zoology, medicine and pharmacy. I check out Tacitus too, to see what he did with Pliny the Younger's description of Mount Vesuvius exploding.

I fall upon the love poetry of Ovid, and his advice, to men and to women, on how to go about the arts of seduction: *Amores* (*The Loves*), *Ars Amatoria* (*The Art of Love*), *Remedia Amoris* (*The Cure for Love*) and the fragmentary *Medicamina Faciei Femineae* (*On Facial Treatment for Ladies*).

In Peter Green's translation Ovid tells young men that they must stick at wooing the love object, even when all seems hopeless, because, in the end, her resistance is futile: 'Birds will sooner fall dumb in springtime, cicadas in summer, or a hunting dog turn his back on a hare, than a lover's bland inducements can fail with a woman.'

He is firm on the matter of women keeping their beauty preparations private—'shut your door, don't reveal the half-finished process…there's a lot men are better not knowing'—and when age has done its damage he is wise:

> When a woman's manners are good, she never fails to attract. Manners indeed are more than half the battle. Time will lay waste your beauty, and your pretty face will be lined with wrinkles. The day will come when you will be sorry you looked at yourself in the mirror, and regret for your vanished beauty will bring you still more wrinkles. But a good disposition is a virtue in

itself, and it is lasting; the burden of the years cannot depress it, and love that is founded on it endures to the end.

And on the matter of wooing older women, whose experience and versatility make up for their lack of youth:

> Don't ask her age, don't inquire under just which consul
> She was born—leave that kind of chore
> To the Censor's office, especially if she is past her girlish
> Prime, and already plucking those first
> White hairs.

Reading these classical writers made it possible to go for several summer holidays without reverting to literary journalism. I rediscovered the joy of browsing. True browsing means that we discover shelves and subjects that we could not have anticipated when we started. And the books we read introduce us to other books, as if we are at a magnificent party of the mind, being ever welcomed by new friends to join in the conversation. An essay on Iceland, 'Paradice', by Eliot Weinberger leads me to read *Independent People* by Iceland's only Nobel Prize winner, Halldór Laxness.

At the height of my work in literary journalism, I avoided bookshops, as they reminded me of the piles of books on and around my desk, and the obligation to choose and to read and to consider and to discuss. I found no rest there, and if I was with people who spent their weekends in beloved bookshops I would wait outside or in the guide-book section or among the foreign language dictionaries or impatiently flip through the CDs just to appease my friends until they had had their fill.

Now I can love bookstores again, and I see their managers as curators not just of what will sell but also of what they think fine and good to read. They are the guardians of the culture, like librarians used to be before the whirring of computers could be heard in the previously silent halls of the hallowed book-lined buildings I remember.

The bookshelves of friends can also be read as the outward expression of the soul within. They are reflections of the accidents of education, and of passions and former interests and ways of leisure. How warming to find a loved book on the shelf of a new friend. How exciting to find books that you have never read. How daunting to find classics that you feel you should have read. You might console yourself with the thought that your friend may not have read them either. We all have shelves of possibility. I have many: *The Essential Tagore*, the Bible, Proust, the complete annotated works of Shakespeare and the collected Freud are just a sample. And I know I should go back to the testing volumes of my impatience, for surely they are called classics for a reason.

Can we really be friends with those who don't love the books that we do? Of course we can, but can we really be friends with those who don't love any books? I'm not so sure of that.

When my daughters were younger I talked about the books I thought they should read, but I didn't use books in the way my mother had, as messages in a bottle, or silent longings to be interpreted. When I had something to say, I said it. I was direct and candid. Sometimes when I say to them, 'Do you know what I think about that?' they chorus 'Yes!' before I have a chance to tell them.

My younger daughter refused to read my recommendations for improving literature; her passion was the *Sweet Valley High* series by Francine Pascal. It sold millions of copies so she was not alone.

But when my older daughter was a teenager, she was a little estranged from me. After she left home, she once returned to recuperate after an illness. I lay on her bed reading aloud a story from my beloved *My Mother's House* by Colette. 'Maternity' is about Colette's mysterious older 'sister with the long hair' who was in a financial dispute with Sido and the Captain, and had 'exiled herself with a husband in a neighbouring house'.

The family hears the sister is about to have a child, and Sido begins to behave erratically. 'One day she seasoned the strawberry tart with salt instead of sugar, and instead of showing distress she met my father's expostulations with a face of stony irony that upset me terribly.'

The night they hear that the sister's labour has begun, Colette observes her mother from an upstairs window, crossing the road and entering the garden at the side of the house in which her daughter's cries of pain could be heard:

> Then I saw my mother grip her own loins with
> desperate hands, spin round and stamp on the ground
> as she began to assist and share, by her low groans, by
> the rocking of her tormented body, by the clasping of
> her unwanted arms, and by all her maternal anguish
> and strength, the anguish and the strength of the
> ungrateful daughter who, so near to her and yet so far
> away, was bringing a child into the world.

My daughter and I cried together on the bed that day, and I still choke up reading the passage now. So maybe I did learn something of the art of semaphore from Mama.

These days I have taken the place of my beloved Mama on the couch. Here I sit among five little grandchildren. One of them can already read, two can pretend to read, and the little twins are just able to hold their first book of ducks and boats and turn the stiff-backed pages, getting ready for their own life in books.

Like me on the floor of the mobile bus library, the older ones lie on their bellies on the bed when they sleep at my house, at first listening to me tell them stories—how many ways can I do Goldilocks?—then to my reading of

Blyton's *The Magic Faraway Tree* and Roald Dahl's *Charlie and the Chocolate Factory*. I do all the voices and they laugh and copy me.

And more recently our eyes are transfixed by my iPad as I read to them from *Alice's Adventures in Wonderland*. Sir John Tenniel's illustrations are strange to them, but familiar to me. Sometimes I paraphrase Lewis Carroll's nineteenth-century language to save from losing the thread of the story through having to explain all the time. But they get the absurdity and the wonder of the adventure, laughing aloud at the idea of Alice drowning herself in her own tears. I am spellbound by their little fingers sweeping along the screen to turn the pages, and the way that even the littlest ones expect all screens to be responsive to their touch.

I know they will grow up with a more diverse reading experience than mine. I had only paper and cardboard and illustrations. Digital reading is already modified by books that show video instead of still pictures, and split screens that show you what others think of your book even before you have read it yourself. Novels have secret spaces where you can read 'backstories' about the characters. You can choose your own story branch and turn reading a book into a kind of game. And as we're in a revolution this is just the beginning. I wonder how much my grandchildren's imaginations might atrophy with so much on offer. Will all the extras result in a subtraction from what the reading experience has been for me? Can we have too much information?

I sometimes read on my tablet computer. Late at night when I see a book I want, and that I must read now, the ease and immediate gratification of digital access suits my temperament. But there are dangers. A *New Yorker* cartoon pictures two men talking under an umbrella at the beach. One has a massive hardback open on his lap and the other says, 'I got tired of *Moby Dick* taunting me from my bookshelf, so I put it on my Kindle and haven't thought of it since.' But while I can be disconcerted by the feeling that, despite the digital bookmark, I don't really know where I am in a book, I enjoy the idea of carrying a library around with me. I have become my own mobile bus library.

But, in the end, the books that surround me are the books that made me, through my reading (and misreading) of them; they fall in piles on my desk, they stack behind me on my shelves, they surprise me every time I look for one and find ten more I had forgotten about. I love their covers, their weight and their substance. And like the child I was, with the key to the world that reading gave me, it is still exciting for me to find a new book, open it at the first page and plunge in, head first, heart deep.

# Acknowledgments

In a life, some years are harder than others. Thank you Penny Hueston, Alison Arnold, Jane Novak and Chong Wengho from Text Publishing for welcoming me to your fine table, and for helping my work to sing.

And to Michael Heyward, your impeccable judgement and ability to magic a book from the murky depths is legendary. I join the league of grateful writers.

And to my family, who understand only too well the hazards of being related to a writer.

And to the writers who made me what I am.

# Book List

*The South Pole: An Account of the Norwegian Antarctic Expedition in the* Fram, *1910–1912* by Roald Amundsen

*The Red Shoes* by Hans Christian Andersen

*I, Robot* by Isaac Asimov

*Home Management: Volume 1*, edited by Alison Barnes

*The Second Sex* by Simone de Beauvoir

*Gathering Evidence: A Memoir* and *My Prizes: An Accounting* by Thomas Bernhard

*The Magic Faraway Tree, Noddy Goes to Toyland, Here Comes Noddy Again, Be Brave Little Noddy!, Do Look Out Noddy!* and *Noddy Gets into Trouble* by Enid Blyton

*Stories in an almost Classical Mode* by Harold Brodkey

*Living Souls* by Dmitry Bykov

*Auto-da-Fé* by Elias Canetti

*Alice's Adventures in Wonderland* by Lewis Carroll

*Silent Spring* by Rachel Carson

*The Worst Journey in the World* by Apsley Cherry-Garrard

*The Rime of the Ancient Mariner* by Samuel Taylor Coleridge

*Cheri, Claudine at School, The Vagabond, My Mother's House*
   and *Sido* by Colette

*The Red Badge of Courage* by Stephen Crane

*Charlie and the Chocolate Factory* by Roald Dahl

*The Origin of Species* by Charles Darwin

*Water Log: A Swimmer's Journey through Britain* and *Wildwood:*
   *A Journey through Trees* by Roger Deakin

*Robinson Crusoe* by Daniel Defoe

*House of Dolls* by Yehiel De-Nur

*Check Your Own I.Q.* by Hans Eysenck

*Madame Bovary* by Gustave Flaubert

*A Passage to India* by E. M. Forster

*The Diary of a Young Girl* by Anne Frank

*Margaret Mead and Samoa: The Making and Unmaking of an*
   *Anthropological Myth* by Derek Freeman

*The Feminine Mystique* by Betty Friedan

*The Prophet* by Khalil Gibran

*Chaos: Making a New Science* by James Gleick

*Faust* and *The Sorrows of Young Werther* by Johann Goethe

*The Wind in the Willows by* Kenneth Grahame

*The Heart of the Matter* and *Brighton Rock* by Graham Greene

*The Diary of a Nobody* by George and Weedon Grossmith

*The Watch Tower* by Elizabeth Harrower

*The Good Soldier Švejk* by Jaroslav Hašek

*A Brief History of Time: From the Big Bang to Black Holes* by Stephen Hawking

*Catch-22* and *Now and Then* by Joseph Heller

*The Histories* by Herodotus

*Siddhartha* by Hermann Hesse

*The Kon-Tiki Expedition: By Raft across the South Seas* by Thor Heyerdahl

*Lost Horizon* by James Hilton

*Leviathan or, The Whale* by Philip Hoare

*The Iliad* and *The Odyssey* by Homer

*Footsteps: Adventures of a Romantic Biographer* and *The Age of Wonder: How the Romantic Generation Discovered the Beauty and Terror of Science* by Richard Holmes

*Rogue Male* by Geoffrey Household

*Brave New World* by Aldous Huxley

*Tales of the Alhambra* by Washington Irving

*Ulysses* by James Joyce

*The Trial* and *Metamorphosis* by Franz Kafka

*The Emperor: Downfall of an Autocrat*, *The Soccer War*, *Another Day of Life*, *Imperium*, *Shah of Shahs*, *The Shadow of the Sun* and *Travels with Herodotus* by Ryszard Kapuściński

*On Reading* by André Kertész

*The Water-Babies: A Fairy Tale for a Land-Baby* by Charles Kingsley

*Lady Chatterley's Lover* and *Women in Love* by D. H. Lawrence

*Independent People* by Halldór Laxness

*The Mind of a Mnemonist: A Little Book about a Vast Memory* and *The Man with a Shattered World: The History of a Brain Wound* by A. R. Luria

*The Group* by Mary McCarthy

# Book List

*Coming into the Country* by John McPhee

*One Hundred Years of Solitude* by Gabriel García Márquez

*The Communist Manifesto* and *Collected Works of Marx and Engels* by Karl Marx and Friedrich Engels

*Growing Up in New Guinea* and *Coming of Age in Samoa* by Margaret Mead

*The Children's Encyclopaedia* by Arthur Mee

*Moby-Dick or The Whale* by Herman Melville

*Tropic of Cancer* and *Tropic of Capricorn* by Henry Miller

*Sisterhood Is Powerful: An Anthology of Writings from the Women's Liberation Movement*, edited by Robin Morgan

*The Naked Ape* by Desmond Morris

*The Tale of Genji* by Murusaki Shikibu

*Farthest North: Being the Record of a Voyage of Exploration of the Ship 'Fram' 1893–96* by Fridtjof Nansen

*Nineteen Eighty-Four, Animal Farm, Down and out in Paris and London, The Road to Wigan Pier* and *Homage to Catalonia* by George Orwell

*Amores (The Loves), Ars Amatoria (The Art of Love), Remedia Amoris (The Cure for Love), Medicamina Faciei Femineae (On Facial Treatment for Ladies)* and *Metamorphoses* by Ovid

*The Hidden Persuaders* and *The Waste Makers* by Vance Packard

*The Little Disturbances of Man* and *Enormous Changes at the Last Minute* by Grace Paley

*Sweet Valley High* by Francine Pascal

*The Road to Reality: A Complete Guide to the Laws of the Universe* by Roger Penrose

*Natural History* by Pliny the Elder

*The Letters of the Younger Pliny* by Pliny the Younger

*By the Book*

*Faust's Metropolis: A History of Berlin* by Alexandra Richie
*What I Saw: Reports from Berlin, 1920–1933* and *Radetzky
    March* by Joseph Roth
*Portnoy's Complaint* by Philip Roth
*Wings of the Kite-Hawk, Another Country, The Red Highway,
    Journeys to the Interior* by Nicolas Rothwell
*Tête-à-Tête: Simone de Beauvoir of Jean Paul Sartre* by Hazel
    Rowley
*A Leg to Stand On, The Man who Mistook His Wife for a Hat
    and Other Clinical Tales, Uncle Tungsten* and *Awakenings* by
    Oliver Sacks
*Catcher in the Rye* by J. D. Salinger
*Rosalind Franklin and DNA* by Anne Sayre
*Scott's Last Expedition: The Journals* by Robert Falcon Scott
*Albert Speer: His Battle with Truth* by Gitta Sereny
*South: The Endurance Expedition to Antarctica* by Ernest
    Shackleton
*The Tale of Genji* by Murasaki Shikibu
*Quo Vadis: A Narrative of the Time of Nero* by Henryk
    Sienkiewicz
*The Collected Stories, Enemies: A Love Story* and *The Slave* by
    Isaac Bashevis Singer
*Longitude: The True Story of a Lone Genius who Solved the
    Greatest Scientific Problem of His Time* by Dava Sobel
*Cancer Ward, The First Circle, The Gulag Archipelago* and
    *One Day in the Life of Ivan Denisovich* by Aleksandr
    Solzhenitsyn
*Hills End* by Ivan Southall
*The Man who Loved Children* by Christina Stead
*The Twelve Caesars* by Suetonius

# Book List

*The Essential Tagore* by Rabindranath Tagore

*To a Mountain in Tibet* and *Shadow of the Silk Road* by Colin
   Thubron

*The Third Wave* by Alvin Toffler

*The Mountain People* by Colin Turnbull

*Adventures of Huckleberry Finn* by Mark Twain

*Kama Sutra* by Vatsyayana, translated by Sir Richard Burton

*The Double Helix: A Personal Account of the Discovery of the
   Structure of DNA* by James D. Watson

*Down among the Women* by Fay Weldon

*Cassell's Book of Knowledge,* Harold F. B. Wheeler

*A Fringe of Leaves* and *Riders in the Chariot* by Patrick White

*The Happy Prince* by Oscar Wilde

*Selected Poems* by Yevgeny Yevtushenko

*Arabian Nights*

*Beowulf*

The Bible

*The Faber Book of Reportage*

*The Icelandic Sagas*

The *John and Betty* books

*The Little Red Hen*

*The Mabinogion*

*The Mahabharata*

Sarajevo Haggadah

*Victorian Readers*—'A Brave Australian Girl' by Anonymous,
   'The Drover's Wife' by Henry Lawson, 'Clancy of the
   Overflow' by Banjo Paterson, 'Bell-birds' by Henry
   Kendall, 'My Country' by Dorothea Mackellar

# Index

# Index

# Index